BULLYING
IN BRITAIN

TESTIMONIES FROM TEENAGERS

By

Adrienne Katz, Ann Buchanan
& Victoria Bream

Listening and responding to young people

Published by Young Voice 2001

Registered charity no: 1078319

12 Bridge Gardens East Molesey, Surrey, KT8 9HU

Copyright Adrienne Katz, Ann Buchanan and Victoria Bream

Adrienne Katz, Ann Buchanan and Victoria Bream assert the moral right
to be identified as the authors of this work.

A catalogue record for this work is available from

The British Library.

ISBN 1- 903456- 01- 0

Designed by Profile Design

Printed in Great Britain by PPG

"A bully's like a king. You rule the playground until someone bullying you takes over. You are deposed."

Male 13 Herts

"Anyone can be a victim of bullying. It happened to me at school, no one is immune. It was unacceptable then and it's unacceptable now."

Jeremy Paxman

"As you can imagine with a name like Love I didn't stand a chance and was badly bullied every day until I left school at 15. My message is don't despair. Once I got away from that environment I prospered and have been very successful."

Best wishes Ray Love, local councillor and former magistrate

Acknowledgements

This study was made possible by support from The Gulbenkian Foundation

 CALOUSTE GULBENKIAN FOUNDATION

The report was produced with support from The Network Foundation and HSBC Bank plc

This study would not have happened without the 7000 young people who took part in the surveys and those who had the courage to speak out in the interviews. We thank each one. We wish to thank all the teachers, youth workers and countless other volunteers who helped make it possible for so many young people to take part.

We acknowledge with gratitude the following for their support in 1996 and 1998 when some of the data used here was collected:
The 'Girlstalk' questionnaire 1996 – distribution: Express Newspapers, The 'Can-do Girls' report – sponsorship: The Body Shop, HSBC. The 'Tomorrow's Men' survey 1998 – distribution: Express Newspapers. 'Leading Lads', research and report: TOPMAN. 'What Sons Say' 1998, HSBC. We are indebted to Sky TV for permission to include data from the 2000 Study, 'Reach For The Sky'.

Photographs contain models, whom we thank. The words in quotations are not attributed to them.

Photographs by Louise Lewer.
Except for: pages 46, 56, 60 by David Hoffman, pages 18, 56, 58 by David Cowlard and page 36 by Neil Turner, pages 22, 55 by Yves Salmon.
Design by Profile Design, Chichester.
Printed by PPG.

This report represents the work of an association between Young Voice and The Centre for Research into Parenting and Children, at the Department of Social Policy and Social Work, University of Oxford. The project was devised and co-ordinated by Adrienne Katz, who wrote the report. The research team was led by Ann Buchanan.

January 2001

through consultation and agreement, negotiation and co-operation. It may re-negotiate this bullying definition at times and the definitions will no doubt vary as indeed they do within research on bullying. This project has had to draw its own line.

Young people in interviews insisted that some mild levels of bullying had to be 'taken' to earn respect. Respondents were divided into three groups: one group were severely bullied; the middle group had been bullied less severely and the third group, mildly or never.

By comparing the two extremes – those bullied 'severely' and 'mildly or never', we are able to see a profile of the differences that were found between these two pole positions. On page 73 we show the questions used to construct and define these groups, and in Chapter 9, "What we know from research", the reader will find some definitions of bullying found in research elsewhere.

"A bully – they can probe for weak points. Some people will make fun of me and tease, it might seem as if we're picking on each other, but if you understand each other you can have a laugh and banter. There are times when you're not in the mood. A good friend can identify with that – a bully goes over the top."
Male 17.

"Bullying is the intentional abuse of power by an individual or a group with the intent and motivation to cause distress to another individual or group. It may occur frequently or infrequently, regularly or irregularly."[1]

"Bullying is aggressive behaviour with certain special characteristics such as repetitiveness and an asymmetric power relationship."[2]

"Bullying is the persistent, wilful, conscious desire to hurt another and put that person under stress."[3]

THOSE WHO WERE BULLIED

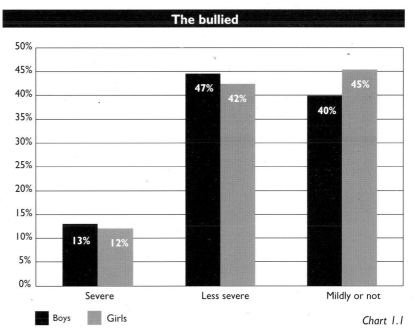

Chart 1.1

- Of 1344 boys who replied to the boys' survey, 13% had been severely bullied.
- 47% had been less severely bullied.
- 40% had been bullied 'mildly' or 'never'.
- Of the 3000 girls, 12% had been severely bullied,
- 42% less severely
- 45% mildly or not bullied.

- **This means that those who are bullied constitute more than half of all children in our schools.**

Types of bullying

To divide the sample into three groups according to the severity of the bullying they had experienced, several questions were grouped together. Questions on being physically attacked, threatened with violence and being picked on by a group were used. The severely bullied group had experienced 'a lot' of these types of bullying.

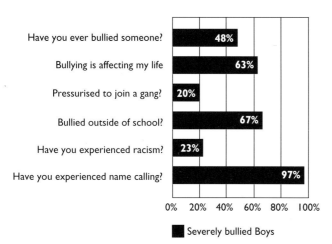

Severely bullied boys' experiences in addition to physical attacks, threats and being picked on by a group

Have you ever bullied someone?	48%
Bullying is affecting my life	63%
Pressurised to join a gang?	20%
Bullied outside of school?	67%
Have you experienced racism?	23%
Have you experienced name calling?	97%

■ Severely bullied Boys

Chart 1.2

Young people also suffered a wide range of other types of victimisation in addition to these:

Girls' severe bullying tactics include blackmail, name-calling and racism along with deliberate exclusion.

Severely bullied boys also report name-calling and racism, but in addition, boys are more likely to be bullied outside school and to be pressurised to join a gang.

Nearly two thirds of those in the severely bullied group felt that bullying was 'affecting their lives' compared to only 4% in the less severe group. But this awareness of how bullying affected their lives, was not found only amongst victims. Almost a quarter of the bullies (as shown in Chart 1.5) also realised that bullying affected their lives.

Severely bullied girls' experiences in addition to being physically attacked, threats and being picked on by a group

Have you been deliberately left out?	87%
Have you experienced blackmail?	45%
Have you bullied someone?	35%
Have you experienced racism?	23%
Have you experienced name calling?	98%

■ Girls

Chart 1.3

"I changed school in the end, it was either that or... my life."

Male 16

In interviews it emerged that certain types of bullying became common in particular schools or areas. Stuffing coats down the toilets, stealing clothing and sports kit was especially common where pupils did not have personal lockers. The use of baseball or cricket bats as weapons and in some cases, knives – were described, especially where battles raged between schools or between groups from different estates. 'Little fires' were set and several methods were devised to damage other people's belongings.

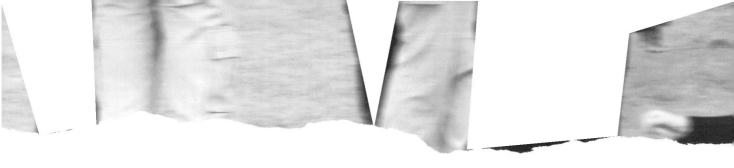

THE BULLIES

 Around a third of all the boys in the entire sample (35%) and a quarter of all the girls (26%) admitted that they had bullied other children. One bully can of course, bully several others. Young people may be reluctant to admit they are bullies, even in this confidential setting. Alternatively they may be unaware when their behaviour crosses the line from 'playing' or 'having a laugh' to bullying. Therefore this figure, alarming as it is, can only hint at the amount of bullying going on.

"It's true people learn to do it themselves. I had a friend who was bullied, when he got to be 18 he began causing fights. It was the only way he knew to get power. Bullies get a buzz off causing fear."

Male prisoner 21.

Have you bullied someone?

Bullies

	Boys		Girls	
80%				
60%		63%		73%
40%				
20%	35%		26%	
0%				

■ A little/A lot ■ Mild/Never

Chart 1.4

There are many paths by which people become bullies and they are complex. These include learned behaviour and unconscious adaptations, which have been described by researchers and professionals working with young people. Space permits us to outline only a few: Some children absorb the message that people appear to get power and adulation by bullying. Others resort to bullying to finally get revenge - or to reduce powerlessness and frustration.

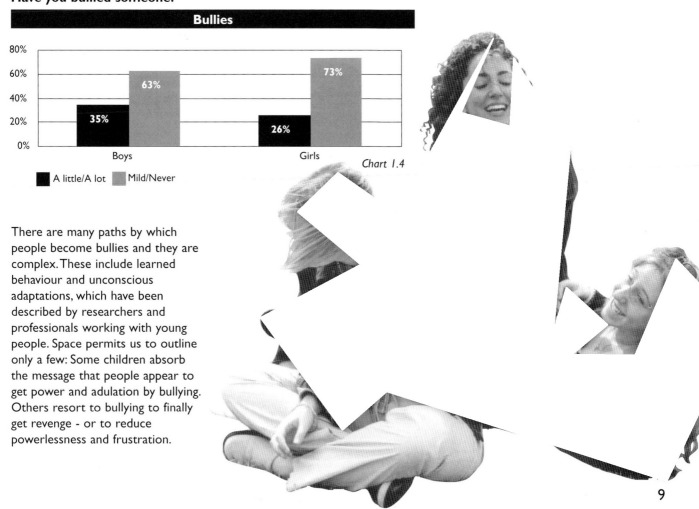

A child might identify with the aggressor and by imitating this aggression, transform himself from the person threatened, into the one who makes the threat.[4] Of course, attack can seem the best form of defence if no alternative skills are taught. A child might bully at a time of great change in his life – such as family break up, bereavement, or a move to a new home. Finding herself in a new threatening social situation, amid feelings of anger and distress, a child might begin to bully. Victims can turn into bullies. 'Aggressive victims' as these individuals are called, can be hardest of all to help.[5]

The bullies' experience – a world of attacks

There was a strong relationship between being bullied and being a bully oneself. Unlike non-bullies, bullies lived in a world of attacks. Significantly more bullies of both sexes, had been physically attacked in school, been made to give up money, threatened with violence, called names, experienced racism

"I saw these 14-15 year olds screaming and shouting on the common, they were pushing and shoving each other. I went in there and said 'What the hell's going on?' It was four against one – a coloured guy. It didn't seem a racist thing, one guy thought he'd stolen a bag and 'phone. To start off with they told me to f... off. Then they came into the school and sorted it out."

Male 17 Peer supporter

and been picked on. But despite this, the levels of stress they reported were lower than the stress levels of the victims. These fights may have been consequences of their bullying actions, or they may have led them to bully, we do not know.

Although some experiences were common to both bullies and victims, there was a noticeable difference of degree: Nearly all the victims and the bullies had been called names, but asking whether they had been bullied outside school or been pressured to join a gang, revealed stark differences.

More than two thirds of the severely bullied boys had been bullied outside school, compared to under a third of male bullies. 20% of the severely bullied boys had been pressurised to join a gang compared to only 12% of male bullies. This may suggest that the most severe forms of bullying are taking place outside school and out of sight of teachers. Some bullies realise that bullying is having an impact on their lives, but these self aware bullies represent fewer than a quarter of their group, compared to nearly two thirds of the severely bullied boys (Chart 1.5).

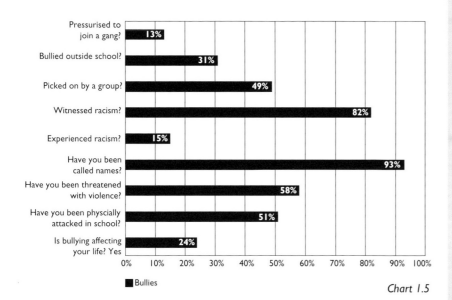

Boy Bullies' experience of being bullied

- Pressurised to join a gang? **13%**
- Bullied outside school? **31%**
- Picked on by a group? **49%**
- Witnessed racism? **82%**
- Experienced racism? **15%**
- Have you been called names? **93%**
- Have you been threatened with violence? **58%**
- Have you been physcially attacked in school? **51%**
- Is bullying affecting your life? Yes **24%**

■ Bullies

Chart 1.5

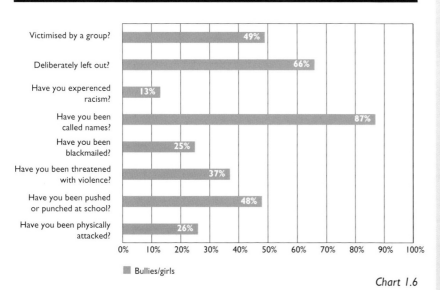

Girl Bullies' experience of being bullied

- Victimised by a group? **49%**
- Deliberately left out? **66%**
- Have you experenced racism? **13%**
- Have you been called names? **87%**
- Have you been blackmailed? **25%**
- Have you been threatened with violence? **37%**
- Have you been pushed or punched at school? **48%**
- Have you been physically attacked? **26%**

■ Bullies/girls

Chart 1.6

87% of girl bullies were called names, two thirds were deliberately left out and almost half get pushed around and a similar number feel victimised.

"Schools reduce bullying and it goes outside. There's more of it now and it's more violent. They should do something about violence in general. Like stricter laws – they should say it's not gonna be tolerated."

Male 16 Newcastle.

Questions for classroom debate:

What is going on in our community? How hidden is it? How do we monitor it? Does the school need to act with the community to reduce bullying outside school? Do local conditions allow bullying to flourish? What can be done to reduce physical violence and create a supportive school within a local multi-agency strategy? How can we involve parents?

Summary

Bullying is widespread. The bullied often admit to bullying others.

- More than half of all young people had been bullied. More than one in 10 had experienced severe levels of bullying including physical violence.
- Almost all children had experienced some types of bullying such as name-calling.
- Bullying was said to be 'affecting my life' by 2/3 of the severely bullied teenagers and also by nearly a quarter of the boys who bullied other people
- More than half of the male bullies and a quarter of the girl bullies had experienced physical violence in school.
- More than two thirds of severely bullied boys have been bullied outside of school.
- 87% of girl bullies had been called names, two thirds had been deliberately left out and almost half had been victimised by a group in addition to being pushed or punched.
- One in five boys who'd been severely bullied felt pressurised to join a gang.
- Girls tended to use blackmail, name calling, exclusion and racism.

"Now they send sick messages to your mobile."

Girl 11

[1] Durham Anti-Bullying Policy Guidelines Durham County Council

[2] Olweus, D. 1993

[3] Countering Bullying Unit UWIC

[4] Freud, Anna, The Ego & Mechanisms of Defence, Hogarth Press with Inst of Psychiatry, 1942 'Identification with the Aggressor'

[5] Cowie, H. 2000 Aggression & Bullying behaviour in children & adolescents. Roehampton Institute London. Boswell & Olweus, D. 1978 Violent Children & Adolescents. Bergen.

What types of families do they come from?

Young victims come from all types of families, yet the figures suggest that young people were less likely to be severely bullied if they lived with both their parents. There are certainly other factors at work, for the study also found that amongst the severely bullied boys, nearly two thirds did indeed live with both parents. Nevertheless it seems that severely bullied boys are more likely than other teenage boys to be living with one parent or a parent and a stepfamily. A number of children may feel especially vulnerable caught up in the maelstrom of family problems, which in turn, are causing them to be withdrawn or angry and less sociable with their peers. Severely bullied girls were far more likely to say they lived with 'a woman who is not my mum' when compared to girls who weren't bullied. In previous work on this girls' dataset, mothers were seen as the first source of emotional support for girls, and where this was lacking, girls' self-esteem was more likely to be low.[1]

"It's hard, it's very difficult. I've got to be able to look after myself. Mum and Dad are divorcing. Better to get someone older and seen in the area to sort it out."

Male 16 living in a B&B

Who do bullied girls live with?

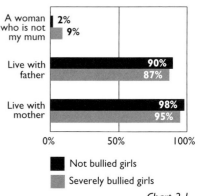

- A woman who is not my mum: 2% / 9%
- Live with father: 90% / 87%
- Live with mother: 98% / 95%

0%   50%   100%

■ Not bullied girls
■ Severely bullied girls

Chart 2.1

Who do bullied boys live with?

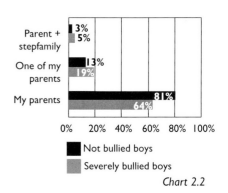

- Parent + stepfamily: 3% / 5%
- One of my parents: 13% / 19%
- My parents: 81% / 64%

0% 20% 40% 60% 80% 100%

■ Not bullied boys
■ Severely bullied boys

Chart 2.2

Working adults

It is always hard to obtain reliable economic information from young people about their parents. These teenagers were asked whether any adults in their household were working, and whether they thought that lack of money had affected their chances. These two questions, with their various components, help form a picture of the economic situation at home.

Compared with non-victims, severely bullied boys and girls reported significantly fewer working adults in their households. More than five times as many boys and three times as many girls also felt that lack of money had affected their life chances. (Bullied boys 22% vs 4%. Bullied girls 9% vs 3%). In the consumerist world of teenagers, not having the same clothes, music or money for entertainment can be divisive.

Worries about parents

Large numbers of children felt generally anxious or protective about their parents: 26% of all boys and 79% of all girls felt anxious about at least one parent. This was more marked among teenagers who'd been severely bullied than those who hadn't. Severely bullied boys in particular tended to worry about money. They were significantly more anxious about their parents' money situation than non-victims.

Backgrounds

Data on ethnic origin is hard to interpret because the young people's categorizations did not neatly fall into those more generally used for example by the Race Equality Unit at the Home Office[2]. Asking them to describe their background in their own words produced an unwieldy number of categories, but was felt by Young Voice to be more respectful. The classifications given by the young people were then broadly divided into those that suggested they came from a minority group and those that suggested they came from the majority white group.

Of all the pupils who were severely bullied, nearly 12% were from a minority community, and they form 6% of the group that were mildly or never bullied.

Looked at another way: One quarter of the minority group said they were severely bullied,

compared to only 13% of the 'white' teenagers. There was however an encouraging sign, around 40% of both the 'white' and the minority group were in the category 'mildly or never' bullied.

Of all the minority community children, a quarter were severely bullied compared to 13% of the 'white' children.

Religious affiliation was also hard to categorize. These were broadly divided into Christian religions and non-Christian. Of those who were non-Christian 12% were severely bullied, compared to 18% of the Christian group (not shown) but very similar percentages of both told of less severe levels of bullying.

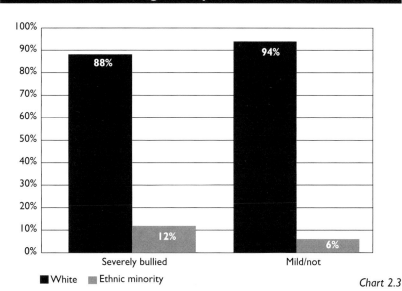

Ethnic Origin of boys who were bullied

- ■ White
- ■ Ethnic minority

Chart 2.3

% of ethnic group reporting severe bullying

- ■ not bullied
- ■ Severely bullied

Chart 2.4

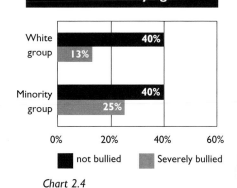

"The only person in the world I'm afraid of is my mum."

Male prisoner 17

What can parents do?

In earlier studies, positive, emotionally nurturing parenting seemed to be protective against depression, suicidal thoughts, being in trouble with the police or hating school. In both girls and boys this positive style of parenting was linked to higher levels of self-esteem or what is described as a 'Can-do' attitude.[3] Can-do girls and boys were less likely to be bullied.

Below, some of these facets of parenting style and family life in relation to being a bully or victim, are explored:

■ **'Family togetherness'**[4] (that is families who frequently ate meals together, visited friends and relatives and went for walks or played sport together) is one of these characteristics.

Three quarters of boys who said they'd only been bullied 'mildly' or 'never', came from families who did things together. More than eighty percent of girl non-victims also came from such families. But there is a warning - parents' lot is never easy: a family style that is too close and overprotective, may be linked with a child who becomes bullied.[5] Finding a balance is, as ever, the key theme, and providing a child with a secure warm family life while encouraging independence and assertiveness is a difficult balancing act.

■ **Do dads protect?**

Another factor that emerged strongly in 'Leading Lads', a study of boys and young men in Britain, was the apparently protective role of fathers[6]. In the present analysis, this finding was confirmed. Although more than 70% of severely bullied boys were living with their fathers, this was significantly fewer than those in the less severe or never bullied groups. Severely bullied boys were also more likely to have a father who had died, or who was absent, living elsewhere (whether they saw him or not) or were more likely to have another man acting as a stepfather.

Similar findings have been shown elsewhere: Children involved in bullying whether as bullies or

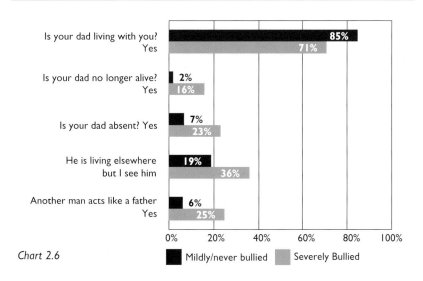

Boys who are bullied and their fathers

Chart 2.6

Legend: ■ Mildly/never bullied ■ Severely Bullied

bully/victims were less likely to have a father at home and more likely to describe family members as 'distant' in a study by Bowers, Smith and Binney.[7] As we have seen above, severely bullied girls were more likely to be living with a woman 'who is not my mum'.

■ **Is living with your Dad enough?**

From the figures in chart 2.6 it seems that a father in the household can be a protective factor, yet there is clearly more to the paternal role than simply physically living together. A number of studies on fathers' influence concentrate on whether or not the family contains a father. But it is possible to be living together and offer a low level of father involvement or to be caring and involved despite not living together.

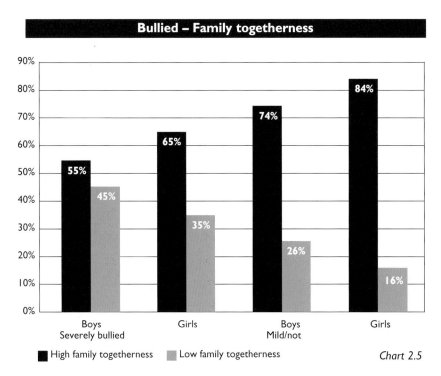

Bullied – Family togetherness

Legend: ■ High family togetherness ■ Low family togetherness

Chart 2.5

■ The quality of fathering.

The study 'Leading Lads', [8]mentioned above, explored the importance of the quality of fathering whether the man was living away from his son or in the same home.

Some fathers were not emotionally available or supportive to their sons despite living together. In 'Leading Lads' links were found between low father involvement and boys who were: depressed, anti-school and in trouble with the police. Young men describing what was termed a 'Dad Deficit', tended to have lower self-esteem than lads with highly involved fathers. In contrast, involved and supportive fathers were associated with sons who had a positive outlook and were optimistic and confident. Their sons were far less likely to be depressed or in trouble with the police and their coping strategies were less antisocial than the Dad Deficit group.

It is naturally easier to be involved when living in the same home as your son, but there were many Dads who, despite this proximity, had sons who were in the 'Dad Deficit' category.

In a discussion of Paternal Deprivation, Anthony Clare refers to a number of other researchers who have studied the effects of what he describes as 'father hunger'. Among the variety of problems that have been linked to this, are school failure or dropping out, emotional and behavioural problems, drug and alcohol problems, poor social skills and control of aggression.[9] In the present study, this theme of involvement was re-visited in relation to bullying and victims.

Boys who weren't bullied were more likely to have an involved father'[10] (that is a Dad who spent time with them; showed an interest in their schoolwork and talked through their worries and concerns with them).

Fathers whether consciously or unconsciously, demonstrate models of masculinity to their sons and can give the impression that manliness consists of 'standing on your own two feet'. In contrast to the involved fathers who provided emotional support, the fathers who felt that their sons should 'fight their own battles', and 'insisted that boys did not cry' were more likely to be linked to sons in the extremely bullied group (not shown).

■ Parenting Style – positive or negative?

Children who weren't bullied were more likely to have parents who were felt to be helpful and loving - parents who were more likely to listen to their sons' or daughters' problems and views, to offer guidance and to have their children's respect. These children were also more likely to think their parents 'lay down the right rules' and 'treat everybody in the family equally.'

But severely bullied boys, said this equal treatment in the family was markedly lacking, when compared to their peers who weren't bullied (36% vs 65%). For bullied boys, life at home was also more likely to be short on parental help (52% vs 76%) and less loving (76% vs 92%) than the home life described by boys who have escaped bullying. (Charts 2.8 and 2.9)

Parents may indeed be less helpful to their teenager, or they may be perceived as such by their son or daughter. Bullied girls say their parents are less helpful. But the difference between these two sets of girls was less dramatic than that shown between the two sets of

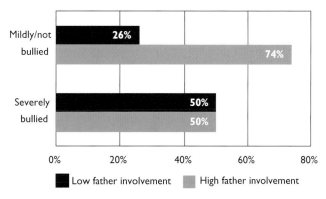

Boys who are bullied and the level of father involvement they report

Mildly/not bullied: 26% (Low father involvement), 74% (High father involvement)

Severely bullied: 50% (Low father involvement), 50% (High father involvement)

■ Low father involvement   ■ High father involvement

Chart 2.7

boys. For males then, this parental help may be valued differently. Girls may look to friends more than boys do for emotional support.

> ## "It's a power trip. It's nice to know there is someone smaller than you, someone you can pick on. I was that person."
>
> Girl 18 Herts

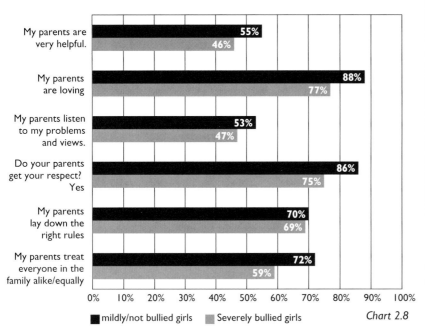

Parenting style and daughters who've been bullied

My parents are very helpful. — 55% (mildly/not bullied girls), 46% (Severely bullied girls)

My parents are loving — 88%, 77%

My parents listen to my problems and views. — 53%, 47%

Do your parents get your respect? Yes — 86%, 75%

My parents lay down the right rules — 70%, 69%

My parents treat everyone in the family alike/equally — 72%, 59%

■ mildly/not bullied girls ■ Severely bullied girls

Chart 2.8

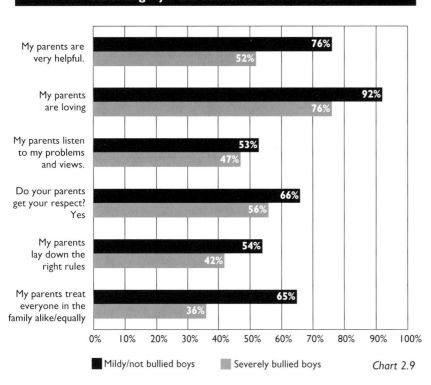

Parenting style and sons who've been bullied

My parents are very helpful. — 76% (Mildly/not bullied boys), 52% (Severely bullied boys)

My parents are loving — 92%, 76%

My parents listen to my problems and views. — 53%, 47%

Do your parents get your respect? Yes — 66%, 56%

My parents lay down the right rules — 54%, 42%

My parents treat everyone in the family alike/equally — 65%, 36%

■ Mildy/not bullied boys ■ Severely bullied boys

Chart 2.9

It is possible that they may develop sensitivity to what they see as unfair treatment – they may be feeling vulnerable and interpret actions rather more acutely than others. But it helps to remember that:

■ A positive style of parenting has a significant relationship to whether a child is bullied or not.

■ Resilience is more likely if the child has good self esteem.

■ At the opposite extreme, various negative parenting characteristics were linked with higher levels of being victimised.

■ Parents of victims were more likely than other parents to be described in two ways - either neglectful, or too controlling and over-protective.

■ Bullied children are more likely than their peers to say they are not treated fairly at home, and their parents don't get their respect.

Compared to children who were not bullied Severely bullied boys were:

■ More than twice as likely to say 'My parents take no notice of me'

■ Nearly five times as likely to say 'My parents treat me like a baby'.

■ Two and a half times more likely to say parents 'try to control everything I do.'

■ Nearly twice as likely to say their parents 'Don't like me to make my own decisions'.

■ Three times more likely to say 'my parents don't get my respect'.

Respect and equal treatment

Although the number of people prepared to say that their parents 'don't get their respect' is quite low, severely bullied boys are three times more likely than their peers to say this. It proved to be even more significant among girls. For both boys and girls the statement 'my parents treat everyone in the family equally' also proved highly significant. Severely bullied young people therefore, may feel that they are being treated unfairly both at home, and by bullies.

Severely bullied girls were:

- Two and a half times more likely to say my parents 'Treat me like a baby', than their peers,
- Twice as likely to say my parents 'Try to control everything I do' and 'They dislike me making my own decisions'.

Taken together, and compared with reports of non-victims, this paints a picture of control, subduing independent thought and initiative.

These findings cannot tell us about cause and effect. Perhaps parents with negative parenting characteristics are responding to young people with more problematic behaviours? But there are links: children who aren't bullied are likely to have parents with a more positive parenting style. This may provide ideas for parents as they try to prepare their children for school and the need to be accepted by their peers.

Summary

Badly bullied boys and girls:

- Come from all types of families, but are less likely to be bullied if they live with both parents.
- Report fewer working adults at home.
- Report lower levels of family togetherness than others.
- Report a more negative parenting style at home

Badly bullied boys are:

- More likely to be living with one parent and step-parent.
- More likely to have a father living elsewhere but in contact, or entirely absent.
- Less likely to report a highly involved supportive father.
- More than five times as likely to say 'lack of money has affected my chances' compared to those not bullied.

Badly bullied girls are:

- More likely to be living with a 'woman who is not my mum'.
- Markedly more anxious about their parents than others
- More than three times as likely to say 'lack of money has affected my chances' compared to those not bullied.

Community

- Of all the children from minority communities, a quarter were severely bullied compared to only 13% of the white children

Family

- 75% of boys and over 80% of girls who are not bullied come from families that do things together.
- Positive, warm, parenting style is linked to those who are not bullied.
- Victims report parents who are controlling, discourage 'making my own decisions', 'lean on me' or 'take no notice of me' and 'treat me like a baby'.
- Severely bullied girls are far more likely to say they plan to bring up their own children very differently from their parents.

Questions for classroom discussion:

How can parents be involved in anti-bullying strategies within schools?

How can parents be given effective support when their child is the bully or is bullied?

How can new parents be part of the negotiating process when an anti-bullying plan is formulated with year seven?

Should parents be provided with information on their child's rights to protection?

If parents have legitimate concerns about safety, what mechanisms can they put in place with other parents to protect children en route to school?

"I didn't want anyone knowing."

Girl 18 Herts

[1] Katz, Buchanan, A. Ten Brinke, JA. (1997) *'Can-do Girls – A Barometer of Change'* Young Voice & Dept of Applied Social Studies, University of Oxford.

[2] Home Office (2000). *Race Equality in Public Service: driving up standards and accounting for progress,*. London: Home Office.

[3] Katz., A. Buchanan, A. Ten Brinke, JA (1997) *'Can-do Girls'* as above.

[4] The appendix gives details of how the family togetherness variable was created.

[5] Smith. P.K. & Myron-Wilson, R. (1998) Parenting and School Bullying

[6] Katz, A. Buchanan. A and McCoy, A. (1999) *Leading Lads,* Young Voice, & The Centre For Research into Parenting and Children, University of Oxford. London.

[7] Bowers, L., Smith P.K. & Binney, V. (1992) *Cohesion and power in the families of children involved in bully.victim problems at school.* Journal of Family Therapy, 14, 371-387

[8] 'Leading Lads,' Katz, A. Buchanan, A. & McCoy, A. 1999 Young Voice as above.

[9] Clare, Anthony. On Men Masculinity in Crisis, Chatto & Windus 2000 Effects of Paternal deprivation p167

[10] See the appendix for full definition

THE BULLIES

The family background of the bullies

As we have seen in the previous section, those who were severely bullied came from all types of families but with some marked differences from those who were not singled out by bullies. Here the family lives of the bullies themselves come under scrutiny. Children who were bullies also came from all sorts of families, but fewer significant differences in family type emerged between the boy bullies and the boys who did not bully. Girls who bullied others, on the other hand were more likely to have a stepfather or another man who acted like a father.

There were no significant differences between the bullies and the non-bullies as far as working adults in the household were concerned. Although it emerged that girl bullies, but not boys, were twice as likely to feel that lack of money had affected their chances.

Compared to victims, a similar proportion, (around half of the boy bullies and a quarter of the girls) were anxious about their parents, but there was little difference between those who had bullied and those who hadn't amongst both boys and girls.

Ethnic background had little influence on whether people did or did not bully.

Discussion: What about parents?

Does the style parents adopt in relation to their child rearing, play a part? This question is naturally being debated as much among parents themselves as those working with parents and making policy. Studies of school anti-bullying interventions by Smith and Myron-Wilson have shown that levels of bullying can be reduced but not eradicated from schools. They suggest this may be because bullying has its origins in parenting as well as in the school environment.[1]

In Britain, with a recent expansion of parenting groups and classes, there are widespread efforts to help parents become aware of 'Positive Parenting' methods. Despite this, a debate still rages on whether physical punishment of children by parents should be banned. This has come about because of a ruling of the European Court of Human Rights in September 1998, which condemned the current protection offered to children by UK law. Children can be brought up with warmth, clear boundaries, fair rules and respect. They need to be listened to, and to make their views heard. This non-violent yet firm style of parenting is often described as 'authoritative' parenting versus 'authoritarian' parenting. The latter is harsh, controlling and often uses physical punishment.

'I think when adults have a first child they don't know how to raise it well. If they are doing it wrong- shouting and smacking – then the kid takes it out on other people. It depends how severe it is. The friends they hang around with influence them.'

Boy, 13 Herts

The urgency of this debate is clear – particularly in relation to bullying. Several studies in Europe, Australia and the US have linked violent behaviour and harsh discipline in parents with bullying - and over-protective parents with victimization.[2]

The 'smacking' debate in Britain over physical punishment has not focused as such on bullying, yet parents' example and influence is a major factor in children's socializing.

Peer aggression has been linked to aspects of parenting – such as lack of warmth, punitive and inconsistent discipline and lax monitoring of the child's activities.[3] Anna Freud[4] has described how some children in an adaptive way imitate the aggressor, in an attempt to become not the one who is at risk but the one who threatens.

In other studies, certain parenting/family characteristics appear to be associated with concerning behaviours. These include work by Sweeting & West[5] in the West of Scotland and a study of boys and young men at risk of depression and suicide[6] undertaken by Katz & Buchanan, for The Samaritans. Adult violence for example, was significantly linked to depression and suicidal thoughts in young men. Many of them in turn admitted to coping strategies that involved 'picking fights' or 'smashing

things up'. In a paper also based on this dataset, Eirini Flouri found that father involvement was an effective buffer against depression in adolescents from disrupted families.[7]

Physical punishment and aggressive children

Arguing that physical punishment increases the chances of aggression, Christina Lyon concludes after reviewing research over the past 40 years, that findings are remarkably

consistent – there is a 'causal relationship between physical punishment and increased aggressive behaviour.'[8] (Violence is discussed in chapter 6)

"They get a kick out of it bullies, it could be reflecting what's happened to them at home if their father beats them or abuse. It's parents that need talking to."

Male prisoner 21

What this study found

This study confirms, as was shown above with victims, that a key factor is parenting style. Family togetherness was one aspect of this. This was striking: Boys who don't bully are more than twice as likely as male bullies, to live in a family that does things together (72% vs 30%) Girls reflect the same message.

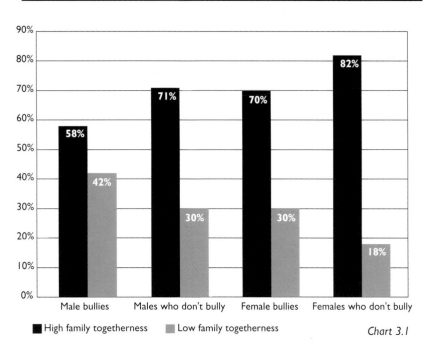

Family togetherness and bullies

	Male bullies	Males who don't bully	Female bullies	Females who don't bully
High family togetherness	58%	71%	70%	82%
Low family togetherness	42%	30%	30%	18%

■ High family togetherness ■ Low family togetherness

Chart 3.1

Fathers

A strong association was found between boys who bully and low father involvement (Chart 3.2). Father involvement describes the quality of interaction between father and child, measured on a number of questions. Involved fathers spent time with their sons; showed an interest in their schoolwork and talked through their worries and concerns with them).

Other writers' views

The unique role of the father in teaching a son to control his strength and aggression is described by family therapist, Steve Biddulph in 'Raising Boys'[9]. Biddulph also discusses the father's role in teaching respect for women, teaching by example and setting a firm framework. Anthony Clare[10] in turn, considers men and violence: "Once upon a time male physical violence may have had a role, in the protection of the species, in deterring attacks, as a means of securing territory and food. In more recent times male violence was still a source of pride and identity. But, in today's society it is no longer either necessary or worthy of admiration: it is increasingly seen as the enemy of culture and civilization. Yet is still exists de-stabilising and shaming us in our streets and in our homes, in the school playgrounds and on the football terraces. The real issue is. What are we going to do about it?"

When comparing the bullies with the non-bullies there was no significant relationship, as to whether their dad was living with them, but significantly more of the bullies had lost their dad (dead or absent) or were living with a man who acted as their father.

> **"The problem is, no matter what the school's policy is, you've gotta get the parents to be saying the same thing – it's no good if they tell their kid to go and beat the daylights out of someone or they beat the daylights out of him themselves."**
>
> Male 17 Newcastle

Fathers involvement and sons who bully

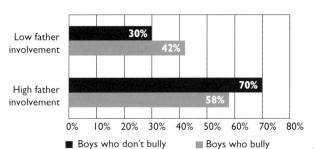

Low father involvement	30% / 42%
High father involvement	70% / 58%

■ Boys who don't bully   ■ Boys who bully

Chart 3.2

> **"My Dad told me to go back and beat the sh... out of them, I was too scared to tell him I was much smaller than them, so I took a knife with me."**
>
> Boy 14

Parenting style and the bullies.

Exploring other parenting characteristics produced similar results to those seen among victims. The non-bullies were more likely to have parents who were seen to be helpful and loving; parents who listened to their sons'/daughters' problems and views and who offered guidance about life and laid down what they saw as the right rules. Those non-bullies were also more likely to live in families where everybody was treated equally and where parents gained respect.

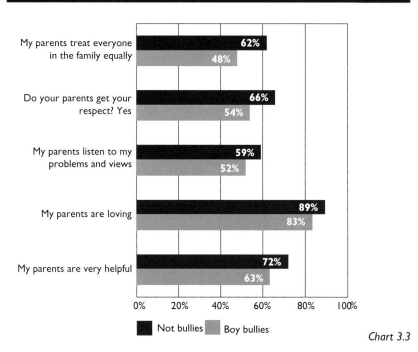

Positive parenting style and boys who don't bully

My parents treat everyone in the family equally — 62% / 48%
Do your parents get your respect? Yes — 66% / 54%
My parents listen to my problems and views — 59% / 52%
My parents are loving — 89% / 83%
My parents are very helpful — 72% / 63%

■ Not bullies ■ Boy bullies

Chart 3.3

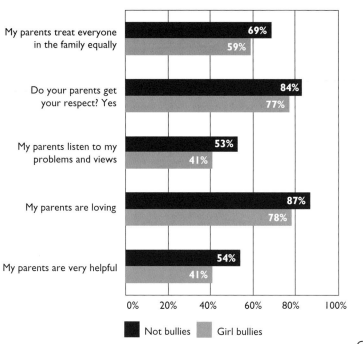

Positive parenting and girls who don't bully

My parents treat everyone in the family equally — 69% / 59%
Do your parents get your respect? Yes — 84% / 77%
My parents listen to my problems and views — 53% / 41%
My parents are loving — 87% / 78%
My parents are very helpful — 54% / 41%

■ Not bullies ■ Girl bullies

Chart 3.4

Negative parenting and bullies

Negative styles of parenting tended to be linked with girls who admitted that they bully other people.

Girl bullies are more likely to be ignored by their parents or treated like a baby. Their parents are likely to try to control everything they do. Girl bullies are not keen to bring up their own children in the same way as their parents, which suggests a criticism. They go further, around one in five of them say they intend to do this 'very differently.' They are very significantly more likely to report that parents take no notice of me, parents don't get my respect, they also don't treat everyone in the family equally; behave lovingly or helpfully.

> ## "I couldn't rely on my mum. I had to fend for myself and you have to be tough."
>
> Girl 14

The differences between the bullies and the non-bullies were generally less pronounced for the boys than the girls. Comparing male bullies and non-bullies, the two most striking differences between their reports are that parents don't 'get their respect' nor do they 'treat everyone in the family equally.'

Girl bullies and their parents

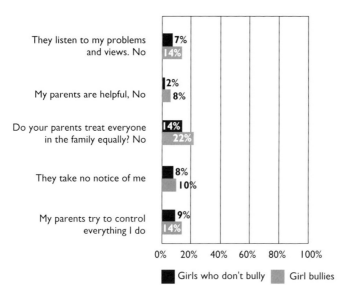

They listen to my problems and views. No — 7% / 14%

My parents are helpful, No — 2% / 8%

Do your parents treat everyone in the family equally? No — 14% / 22%

They take no notice of me — 8% / 10%

My parents try to control everything I do — 9% / 14%

0% 20% 40% 60% 80% 100%

■ Girls who don't bully ■ Girl bullies

Chart 3.5

Boy bullies and their parents

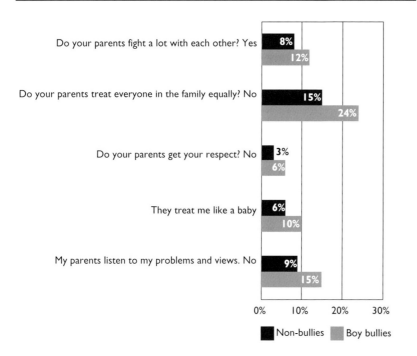

Do your parents fight a lot with each other? Yes — 8% / 12%

Do your parents treat everyone in the family equally? No — 15% / 24%

Do your parents get your respect? No — 3% / 6%

They treat me like a baby — 6% / 10%

My parents listen to my problems and views. No — 9% / 15%

0% 10% 20% 30%

■ Non-bullies ■ Boy bullies

Chart 3.6

"My dad was hit badly when he was a boy. He tries not to lay a hand on me. I respect that."

Male 17 Bradford

Discussion

In 'Violence and Society'[11] the author, Elie Godsi considers the sometimes harsh, uncaring and often violent, world into which some children are born. "Households in which relationships are characterised by tension, discord, aggression or fragmentation are dramatically on the increase, and without doubt this is having profound consequences for children who are caught up in this." He is sensitive to the fact that adults may themselves be weary, unwell or distressed or at the very least irritable under the stresses of excessive work or poverty.

"They used to be bitchy about x in front of me. I never used to say anything. I would just go along with it."

Girl 18 London

The demands of economic survival and uncertainty, he writes, can still be expressed in a kind of tired neglect of parental care and familial time. "Many parents, trying their utmost and with the best will in the world, still end up harming each other and their children in the face of brutal work conditions and financial insecurity." This has led to dramatic increases in the numbers of violent juveniles and children who are excluded from school on account of disruptive unmanageable or violent behaviour - children he suggests, who may be developing this behaviour as a way of expressing themselves in response to unfavourable conditions. Frequently, to make sense of this behaviour, the response is to blame it on biology, to medicalise or pathologise it rather than blame the chaotic conditions in which they are raised. It seems therefore that no consideration of bullying can ignore home life.

Question for classroom debate:

Is aggressive behaviour among teenagers a response to stress and growing up in unfavourable conditions? What would happen if we all took out our frustrations or emotions on one another? How do I want to be treated? Does that help me know how someone else feels? What

works to stop bullying, yet deals with a bully's needs? Is suspension effective? How can clear rules be set and enforced? How do we make sure bullying is not rewarded by power, influence or material things?

(simply raising the bully's self esteem has not been found effective in Norwegian schools, says Professor Dan Olweus.)

> **"A person who is bullied is affected always. Would I intervene? Yeah quite a few times I've stopped a fight – if you're bigger you can. But parents should all tell their kids the same thing in the first place. Some tell kids to hit back and some don't. If you feel strong enough you shouldn't take it."**
>
> Male 15 Twickenham

SUMMARY

Bullies

■ Bullies come from all types of families.

■ Girl bullies were more likely to have a stepfather or other man acting as a father.

■ Girl bullies are twice as likely as non-bullies to feel that 'a lack of money has affected my chances'.

■ A similar proportion of bullies and victims was anxious about their parents

■ The key finding was the relationship with parenting style. Boys who bully were more likely to report unequal treatment within the family and parents who don't get their respect. Their parents also fight a lot with each other. Girls revealed even more pronounced differences than boys between the parenting styles described by bullies and non-bullies, and are less likely to plan to look after their own children in the same way as their own parents.

■ Children who don't bully were more likely to have families who do things together and have an involved father.

[1] Smith, P.K. & Myron-Wilson, R. (1998) Parenting & School Bullying, Clinical Child Psychology and Psychiatry 3, 405-417

[2] Smith, P.K. & Myron Wilson, R as above

[3] Olweus, D. 1980 Familial and temperamental determinants of aggressive behaviour in adolescent boys: a causal analysis. Developmental Psychology 16, 644-660. Dishion, T.J. (1990) The family ecology of boys' peer relations in middle childhood. Child Development 61, 874-892

[4] Freud, Anna, 'The Ego & Mechanisms of Defence', Hogarth Press with Inst of Psychiatry, 1942 'Identification with the Aggressor'.

[5] Sweeting, H. and West, P. (1995) Family Life and Health in Adolescence: a role for culture in the health inequalities debate? Social Science and Medicine, 40, 2, 163-175

[6] Buchanan, A. Katz, A and McCoy, A. (1999) Young Men Speak Out London: the Samaritans.

[7] Flouri, E. Bream, V. and Buchanan, A. 'Paternal involvement and child outcomes in adolescence' Forthcoming. Department of Social Policy and Social Work, University of Oxford

[8] Lyon, C.M. (2000) Loving Smack or Lawful Assault, IPPR London

[9] Biddulph, Steve. Raising Boys, Thorsons London 1998

[10] Clare, Anthony. On Men, Masculinity in Crisis. Chatto and Windus 2000

[11] Godsi, E. (1999) Violence in Society, the reality behind violent crime. Constable, London Elie Godsi is Consultant Clinical Psychologist, Head of Forensic Psychology Nottingham.

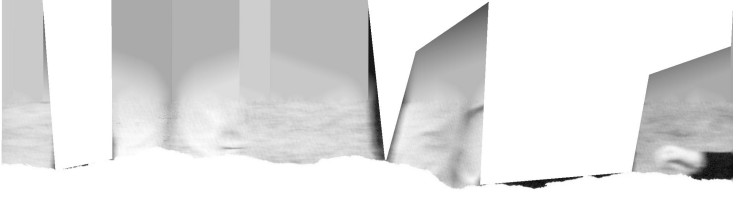

Inner world meets outer reality.

In this chapter we explore links between the inner world of young people and the day-to-day realities of school behaviour. Those in this study are aged between 12-19, a time that can bring confusion and turmoil in any adolescent, when image and identity, belonging and acceptance become all-important. If an intervention is to succeed, it must take into account how these teenagers feel. The ideas below were gathered in interviews and are offered here with the data from surveys.

Discussion – Gender stereotypes – who believes them?

No exploration of any area of emotional life and peer relations among adolescent boys can be complete without asking questions about masculinity and the way it is acted out among teenage boys. As they said – 'You have to be tough even if you're dying inside.'

'Acting like a man' may be the greatest barrier preventing young boys from seeking help. Boys who were severely bullied, were more likely to believe that they have to 'cope with problems alone', that they have to 'match up to one ideal of maleness' and that they 'must be tough to survive'. (Chart 4.1)

These figures suggest that it is unlikely they will readily ask for help without worrying that they will be seen as 'pathetic'. More seriously – that they will feel pathetic. Their worries are valid. Bullies too believe that boys have to conform to one idea of maleness and they have to be tough to survive. As bullies are the enforcers – it is likely that they influence the bullied boys into accepting these unwritten 'rules'.

Efforts to intervene or encourage victims to 'tell someone', will need to take this into account. Any intervention must protect both the self-image of this young person and his image among his peers.

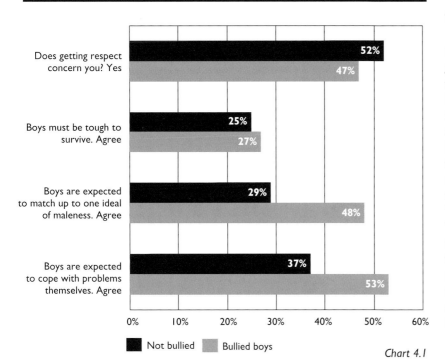

Bullied boys and male stereotypes

Does getting respect concern you? Yes
- Not bullied: 52%
- Bullied boys: 47%

Boys must be tough to survive. Agree
- Not bullied: 25%
- Bullied boys: 27%

Boys are expected to match up to one ideal of maleness. Agree
- Not bullied: 29%
- Bullied boys: 48%

Boys are expected to cope with problems themselves. Agree
- Not bullied: 37%
- Bullied boys: 53%

■ Not bullied ■ Bullied boys

Chart 4.1

Girls – traditional or tough?

Girls who were severely bullied, gave a confusing response. Unlike the vast majority of girls, who believe that 'ideas about how girls behave' are changing – in a direction away from traditional roles. Severely bullied girls are less convinced that this is so. Despite this, they were more likely to believe that girls had to 'put on a tough front' and that 'caring for others held you back'. The latter might be to protect themselves against the hurt that follows when a friend turns bully, rather than like most girls, who said this because they were ambitious and believed that a career might be blocked by caring for a family.

Reporting bullying (dobbing or grassing) is often portrayed as girlishness, thus increasing risk at a time when homophobic bullying is rife. When some schools intervene, it seems the opposite of the intended outcome is achieved. The victim is exposed to more risk due to the way the incident is handled. Certain younger boys, who'd been encouraged to report every incident to the teacher, developed a learned helplessness about dealing with even the slightest name-calling incident on their own. They began to believe that they were wimps and everyone else believed it too. For their part, teachers' responses became dulled if the same child reported what seemed trivial incidents too often. Teachers may also 'believe deep down that a boy should stand on his own two feet.' Peer support may offer alternative ways of tackling this[1].

"I've told the teacher lots of times. Teachers have better things to do they don't wanna know." Boy 15, Liverpool, after saying he goes to the teacher every time anything happens. He now no longer expects anything to happen, but is taking no steps himself to deal with bullying besides repeatedly telling the teacher.

> **"I tell the teacher every time. It happens all the time. The teacher doesn't do anything much. One boy got suspended but it didn't help me. He waited for me out of school… he came to my house and trashed the laundry on the line."**
>
> Boy 15 Liverpool

Boys who weren't bullied were less likely to accept these beliefs about how men act. Using bystanders to turn around the power of the bully, is an alternative put forward in some peer support schemes.

> **"He thinks, oh he looks weak – I could take him – and then they keep doing it. When they think the teacher forgot about it they start up again."**
>
> Boy 16 Liverpool

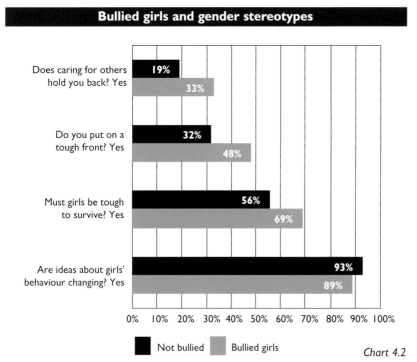

Bullied girls and gender stereotypes

Does caring for others hold you back? Yes
- Not bullied: 19%
- Bullied girls: 33%

Do you put on a tough front? Yes
- Not bullied: 32%
- Bullied girls: 48%

Must girls be tough to survive? Yes
- Not bullied: 56%
- Bullied girls: 69%

Are ideas about girls' behaviour changing? Yes
- Not bullied: 93%
- Bullied girls: 89%

■ Not bullied　　■ Bullied girls

Chart 4.2

What would you tell your younger brother?

When asked in interviews what they would tell a younger brother about dealing with a bully, young people - male and female - unanimously agreed that 'you shouldn't let him (or her) see fear, you shouldn't let him get away with it - even once - because he'll do it again and again.' It was agreed that bullies 'get a buzz out of fear'. If you could act tough, you might escape. They insist you have to avoid looking as though you need help from anywhere else, even if you have enlisted help.

> **"There was this boy – he was bullied. He went home and came back and they got in a fight and fell. When they were found, the boy who was being bullied was on top of the bully. Everyone thought he had knocked him down. Now he gets respect."**
>
> Male 13 London

Causes of stress

For around a quarter of boys and girls who experienced severe bullying, the most important stress in their lives was - not surprisingly - bullying. However, severely bullied children also had a range of other important stresses in their lives.

High numbers of all children were worried about schoolwork and exams, listing it as their number one concern. But bullied boys were less likely to rank this at number one.

For example, 31% of severely bullied boys rated relationships outside the family as their number one stress and 21% listed sexual performance. 31% listed worries about being sexually abused. (Numbers were too low to test for significance and it is likely that, having listed this at all, one would put it at number one.[2]) Homophobic bullying may produce extra anxiety about sexual orientation in severely bullied boys - 39% listed it as a cause of stress compared to 13% of boys who weren't bullied. On the other hand they may be worried about this already and the bullying may be a consequence or additional stress.

Severely bullied boys were:

■ Much more likely to rate alcohol a number one source of stress (63% vs 14%)

■ Significantly more worried about getting a girl pregnant (58% vs 12%)

■ More likely to list drugs as their prime concern (46%vs 14%).

■ More than a third were worried about their sexual orientation −39% vs 13%

Worries about how you look, or conflict at home were not found to be significant. (Chart 4.3)

Girls

Compared to girls who were hardly ever bullied, severely bullied girls worried less about schoolwork (46% vs 59%) and more about their relationships outside the family. (26% vs 14%) They were twice as likely to select worry about sexual abuse, but numbers were small and they were four times more likely to worry about drugs.

Bullied girls:

■ Were twice as likely to say that bullying was their number one cause of stress.

■ Were slightly more likely to list conflict at home.

■ More than twice as likely to list being hit.

■ 17% compared to 10% listed worry about being sexually abused.

Otherwise they did not fear much or admit to many causes of stress - being strikingly less likely than all other girls to say they worried about being followed and attacked. However like other girls, they were worried about getting pregnant, pre menstrual tension, alcohol, sex or parents divorcing.

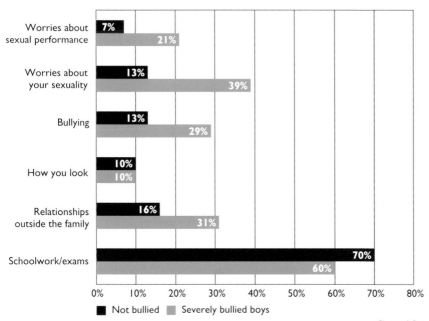

Bullied boys and causes of stress

	Not bullied	Severely bullied boys
Worries about sexual performance	7%	21%
Worries about your sexuality	13%	39%
Bullying	13%	29%
How you look	10%	10%
Relationships outside the family	16%	31%
Schoolwork/exams	70%	60%

Chart 4.3

This is a view shared by only around a third of non-victims. These replies show two pathways, one towards withdrawing and staying in your room, the other to explode with rage and impulsive behaviour which may be anti-social and lead into further trouble, perhaps with the police.

- Bullied boys are more than three times as likely to take an illegal drug or to pick fights, than boys who aren't bullied badly.
- A quarter would 'stay in my room' if distressed, while only 14% of non-victims chose this strategy.
- Bullied boys are more than twice as likely to smash something, to smoke and to 'go out on my own' than non-victims.

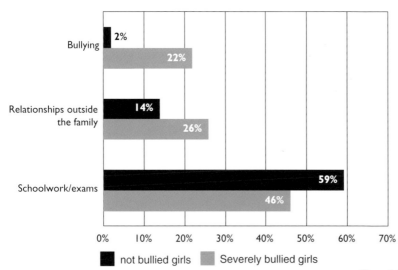

Bullied girls and causes of stress

	not bullied girls	Severely bullied girls
Bullying	2%	22%
Relationships outside the family	14%	26%
Schoolwork/exams	59%	46%

Chart 4.4

"I hated myself, I felt there must be something I'd done wrong or terrible about me for this to happen. I felt ashamed."

Girl 14

Coping strategies

Clues to help adults recognise depression and deal with anti-social behaviour are found in the ways young teenagers said they respond to severe distress.

Bullied boys' coping strategies differed significantly from other young men. The strategies they used most frequently were: keeping things to yourself (30%), staying in your room 24%, getting irritable 21% and going out on your own 20%, but

- 17% felt they would smash something.
- 10% take an illegal drug.
- 9% pick fights.

These actions may fit in with a belief, held by more than half of them - that 'boys are expected to cope with problems themselves'.

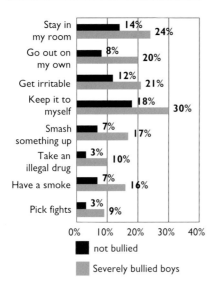

	not bullied	Severely bullied boys
Stay in my room	14%	24%
Go out on my own	8%	20%
Get irritable	12%	21%
Keep it to myself	18%	30%
Smash something up	7%	17%
Take an illegal drug	3%	10%
Have a smoke	7%	16%
Pick fights	3%	9%

■ not bullied
■ Severely bullied boys

Chart 4.5

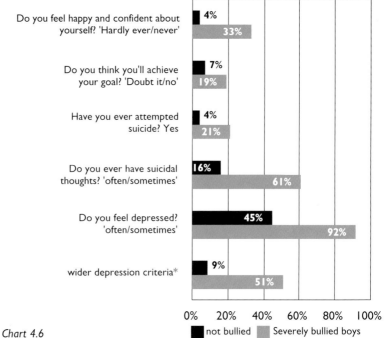

	not bullied	Severely bullied boys
Do you feel happy and confident about yourself? 'Hardly ever/never'	4%	33%
Do you think you'll achieve your goal? 'Doubt it/no'	7%	19%
Have you ever attempted suicide? Yes	4%	21%
Do you ever have suicidal thoughts? 'often/sometimes'	16%	61%
Do you feel depressed? 'often/sometimes'	45%	92%
wider depression criteria*	9%	51%

■ not bullied   ■ Severely bullied boys

Chart 4.6

Consequences?

As this study is only reporting associations, we cannot say for sure what comes first: Are children who are depressed more likely to be bullied? Experience suggests they are. Or are children who are severely bullied more likely to feel depressed and even suicidal? Equally, this is logical to expect.

What the following charts no 4.6 and 4.7 do show however, is that when you compare severely bullied girls and boys with those who are not bullied, there are much higher levels of distress amongst the bullied victims. Depression, suicidal thoughts, suicide attempts, and an almost pervasive sense of hopelessness, particularly for the boys, permeate their replies: A sad finding was that although one in five of the severely bullied boys had attempted suicide, nearly one in three of the less severely bullied had also attempted suicide. There were rather high levels of depression amongst this group.

NOTE: In the survey taken in 1996 on girls' views, we did not have an opportunity to ask about suicidal

thoughts. However returning to some of these issues in 2000, we did so. Those girls who reported having suicidal thoughts 'often', were found in the following groups: 24% of girls who had experienced a lot of violence from bullies. 20% of girls who had been bullied a lot in school, 21% of girls who'd bullied others.

Those girls who said they had made an attempt were looked at. Bullies and their targets revealed rates that are cause for concern. 32% of girl bullies said they had done so, as had

29% of those who had experienced a lot of violence from bullies, and this was sadly also true of 27% who had been bullied 'a lot' in school.

"He was born confident, but what those people did to him was unspeakable, he lost his confidence altogether" a mother talking about her son who had been badly bullied over a long period.

"I felt the whole world was crushing me – there was nowhere to go to be away from this torture."

14 boy

28

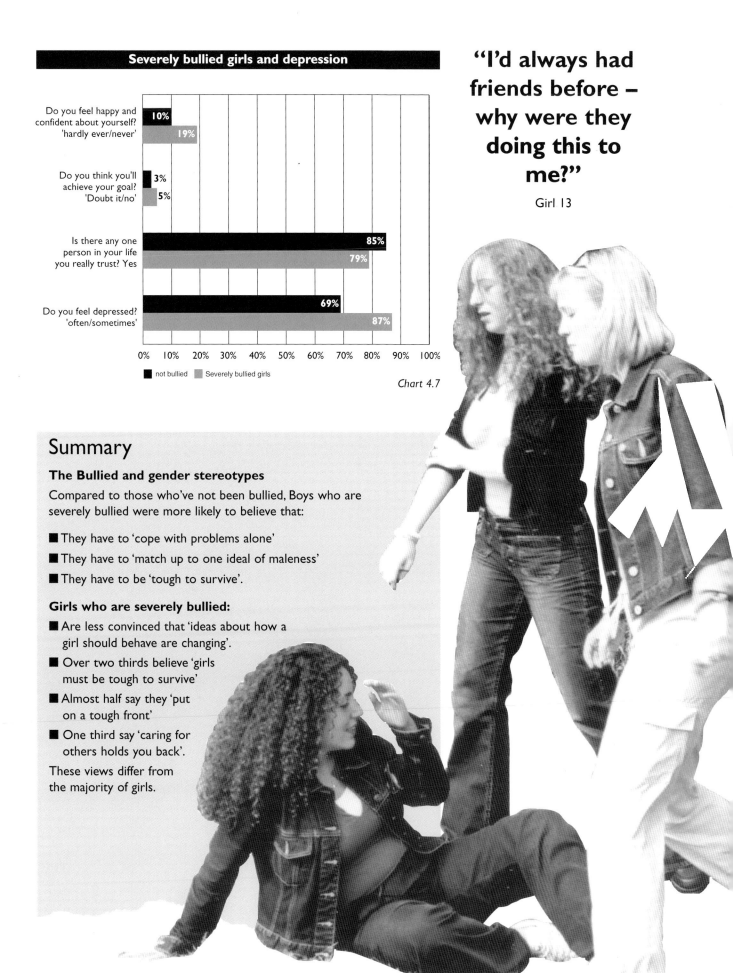

Severely bullied girls and depression

Do you feel happy and confident about yourself? 'hardly ever/never'
- not bullied: 10%
- Severely bullied girls: 19%

Do you think you'll achieve your goal? 'Doubt it/no'
- not bullied: 3%
- Severely bullied girls: 5%

Is there any one person in your life you really trust? Yes
- not bullied: 85%
- Severely bullied girls: 79%

Do you feel depressed? 'often/sometimes'
- not bullied: 69%
- Severely bullied girls: 87%

■ not bullied   ■ Severely bullied girls

Chart 4.7

"I'd always had friends before – why were they doing this to me?"

Girl 13

Summary

The Bullied and gender stereotypes

Compared to those who've not been bullied, Boys who are severely bullied were more likely to believe that:

■ They have to 'cope with problems alone'

■ They have to 'match up to one ideal of maleness'

■ They have to be 'tough to survive'.

Girls who are severely bullied:

■ Are less convinced that 'ideas about how a girl should behave are changing'.

■ Over two thirds believe 'girls must be tough to survive'

■ Almost half say they 'put on a tough front'

■ One third say 'caring for others holds you back'.

These views differ from the majority of girls.

Stress.

Around a quarter of all the young people rated bullying as the most important stress in their lives while most young people rated worry about schoolwork as their main worry. Bullied pupils had other concerns too, besides bullying, which were often more worrying to them than schoolwork.

Bullied boys and six top causes of stress

Alcohol was the most frequently selected worry followed by getting a girl pregnant, drugs, sexuality, relationships outside the family, conflict at home

Bullied girls and six top causes of stress

Relationships outside the family was the most frequent worry closely followed by conflict at home, being sexually abused, feeling powerless, bullying and how you look.

The bullied and coping strategies

Apart from keeping it to myself, staying in my room, 17% would smash something, 10% would take an illegal drug and 9% pick fights - a rate three times higher than that of non bullied boys.

(Data on girls' coping strategies has since been collected and will be analysed in future work.)

The bullied and depression.

Being bullied, as might be expected is associated with depression. It is unclear whether depressed people are more likely to be bullied, or whether it is the bullying which causes the depression
Compared to those boys who were not bullied:

■ Severely bullied boys were more than five times as likely to be depressed

■ 61% of these bullied young men had suicidal thoughts

■ One in five had made a suicide attempt

■ Three times as many severely bullied boys don't believe they'll achieve their goal

■ Eight times as many of them hardly ever feel happy and confident about themselves

■ Strikingly, one in three boys reporting less severe bullying had also made a suicide attempt

Compared to those girls who were not bullied:

■ Severely bullied girls were significantly more likely to be depressed

■ They were less likely to have someone in their life they really trust

■ Severely bullied girls are twice as likely to believe they won't achieve their goal

■ They are twice as likely to say they hardly ever feel happy and confident about themselves.

■ More than one in four girls who had experienced violence from bullies had made a suicide attempt*

* figures taken in a separate survey 2000

Questions for classroom debate:

How would you know if your friend was depressed? What do you do when you feel very distressed? Are these actions going to be helpful to you? Are there other coping plans you might think of in advance? Do you have someone you trust? Do you know of any help services for young people you could use? How would you find out about these?

THE BULLIES

THE BULLIES

Bullies and bullied boys alike, accept and live by the myths of masculinity. Images of toughness abound despite the fact that in private, young men admit this is only 'a front'. In contrast to all other young men, bullies and victims were more likely to agree that 'boys are expected to cope with problems themselves'.

But the bullies buy into this image to a slightly lesser extent than the severely bullied boys, maybe because the latter are struggling to live up to it. (bullies 43% vs bullied 53%)

To a greater extent than people who aren't involved with bullying, these two groups – bullies and bullied - also say that they have 'to match up to one idea of maleness.' (Bullies 38% and bullied 49%) The victims it seems are daily made aware of a need to match up to this idea of how men act. It is indeed often the reason they are picked on – for simply not matching up to someone else's yardstick and because homophobic bullying has become so common – it suggests that any deviation from the 'hard man' image is considered effeminate.

"People don't accept me for what I am – I've had to come to terms with myself. I'll never be the school hero – I don't even like football. I hate the lad culture with its bragging about sex and being so hard."

Male 16

Not surprisingly, a highly significant finding for bullies of both sexes was how strongly they felt that they had to be 'tough to survive' and to 'put on a tough front.'

More than a quarter of the girl bullies also believed that 'caring for others held you back.' Many discussions of bullying interventions revolve around the questions of how to teach empathy and foster an ethos of caring within the group. This may be particularly difficult when faced with young people who cannot trust 'caring' because they've been 'let down', 'betrayed' or hurt both by adults and their peers. Rebuilding this trust is a challenge directly tackled by programmes such as Peer Support, Circle Time and Connections.[3]

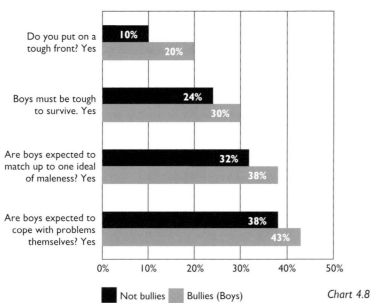

Male bullies and attitudes to masculinity

Do you put on a tough front? Yes
- Not bullies: 10%
- Bullies (Boys): 20%

Boys must be tough to survive. Yes
- Not bullies: 24%
- Bullies (Boys): 30%

Are boys expected to match up to one ideal of maleness? Yes
- Not bullies: 32%
- Bullies (Boys): 38%

Are boys expected to cope with problems themselves? Yes
- Not bullies: 38%
- Bullies (Boys): 43%

■ Not bullies ■ Bullies (Boys)

Chart 4.8

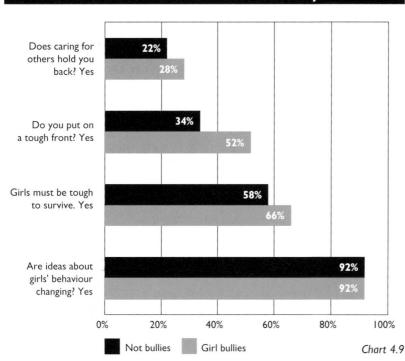

Girl bullies and attitudes to femininity

Does caring for others hold you back? Yes
- Not bullies: 22%
- Girl bullies: 28%

Do you put on a tough front? Yes
- Not bullies: 34%
- Girl bullies: 52%

Girls must be tough to survive. Yes
- Not bullies: 58%
- Girl bullies: 66%

Are ideas about girls' behaviour changing? Yes
- Not bullies: 92%
- Girl bullies: 92%

■ Not bullies ■ Girl bullies

Chart 4.9

Bullies worry too

Clearly the issue of bullying itself worries some bullies: 16% of boys and 14% of girls. Bullies of both sexes rated worrying about schoolwork lower than people who did not bully. Significantly more girl bullies were concerned about their looks than the non-bullies (18% vs 13%) yet they were noticeably less likely to fear being powerless than other young people – their bully status conveyed power. Reducing that power should be one aim of an anti bullying strategy – while bullies retain power they are 'rewarded' for their actions.

Girl bullies differed significantly from non-bullies on causes of stress, such as schoolwork (they cared less) 'how you look' (they cared more) and feeling powerless. Where numbers were too small to test for significance there were nevertheless some interesting results. Bullied girls tended to rank the following causes of stress as their number one worry. In each case the percentage doing so was higher than that of girls who were not bullies.

Bully girls:

■ Were twice as likely to say that bullying was their number one cause of stress.

■ Were slightly more likely to list conflict at home,

■ More than twice as likely to list being hit,

■ 17% compared to 10% listed worry about being sexually abused.

Otherwise they did not fear much or admit to many causes of stress - being strikingly less likely than all other girls to say they worried about being followed and attacked.

Male Bullies' coping strategies tend to be anti-social

The most significant differences between male bullies and non-bullies were the extent to which they used more antisocial type activities to cope with stress. Boys who bully were much more likely to resort to violence – 13% of them felt they would smash something compared to 8% of the non-bullies; 8% compared to 2% felt they would pick fights, 18% compared to 9% felt they would have a drink, 9% compared to 3% felt they would take an illegal drug. When it came to the more pro-social ways of coping with stress, the differences between the bullies and the non-bullies was also significant but the associations tended to be less strong.

Bullies are:

■ Four times as likely to pick fights.

■ Twice as likely to have a drink.

■ Three times as likely to take a drug to relieve distress.

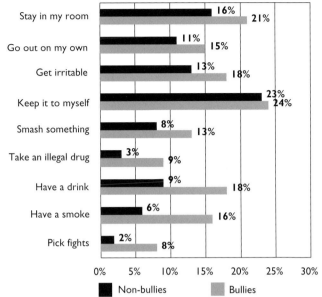

Male bullies and what they do when distressed

Behaviour	Non-bullies	Bullies
Stay in my room	16%	21%
Go out on my own	11%	15%
Get irritable	13%	18%
Keep it to myself	23%	24%
Smash something	8%	13%
Take an illegal drug	3%	9%
Have a drink	9%	18%
Have a smoke	6%	16%
Pick fights	2%	8%

Chart 4.10 — ■ Non-bullies ■ Bullies

Young men who bully are more likely to engage in a destructive or self-destructive way when they are stressed.

[2] 44 people ranked fear of being sexually abused as their top cause of stress. Of these 17 were bullies by their own admission, 27 were non-bullies. As bullies form a group of 469 and boys who don't bully represent 842 of the sample, it is an interesting finding*.

[3] Peer Support, Circle Time and Connections are listed in useful addresses, page 76 In addition see Re-membering Education and the work of Antidote.

[4] 2772 young people surveyed March 2000.

Consequences?

Being a bully was not necessarily a path to happiness. More than eighty per cent of the boy bullies were often or sometimes depressed and this trend was reflected by the girls but to a lesser degree. More than a third of the boy bullies had had suicidal thoughts and 9% had actually attempted suicide. On all measures of distress except depression, bullied people were more distressed than bullies.

*Looking at girls' replies to a more recent dataset (2000) girls who said they'd bullied others also showed a tendency to suicidal thoughts (21%) and alarmingly, almost a third said they'd made an attempt[4]).

Questions for debate:

What is a stereotype? Are fixed ideas about how males and females behave still with us? Do we have to live up to these? Do they limit the person you can be? How far have they changed? Do these stereotypes have a positive or negative effect? What are your choices if you feel very upset or angry? Does they way you handle this help you or make things worse for you?

Summary. The Bullies

The Bullies and Coping strategies

The strategies male bullies use when they are very distressed were the most significant differences between them and the non bullies.

■ Bullies are two and a half times more likely to smash something

■ 4 x more likely to pick fights

■ 2 x more likely to go and have a drink

■ 3 x as likely to have an illegal drug

The bullies and image and gender

In contrast to non-bullies,

■ Bullying girls are far more likely to put on a tough front, and

■ Male bullies are twice as likely to do so.

■ Bullies of both sexes are far more likely to believe 'you have to be tough to survive'.

■ Well over a quarter of girl bullies believe 'caring holds you back'.

Bullies and causes of stress

Compared to non-bullies:

■ Girl bullies worry more about their looks

■ Twice as many girl bullies worry about bullying

■ Although fewer male bullies than non bullies worry about bullying, as many as 16% say it's their number one worry.

Bullies and Depression

■ 38% of boy bullies had suicidal thoughts

■ 9% of boy bullies had attempted suicide

■ Girl bullies were significantly more likely to be depressed than non bullies.

■ 13% of female bullies were hardly ever, or never - happy and confident

■ One in five girl bullies often had suicidal thoughts*

■ Girls who bully are less likely to believe they'll achieve their goal.

Except for depression, on all other measures of distress, the level of distress reported by bullies was generally much less than those who'd been severely bullied.

* from data collected in 2000

"No leper or spy can have suffered so long or so sharply as I did as I struggled to live cheek-by-jowl twenty four hours a day for two years with the shouted taunts and the subtle cruelties of my fellow Etonians...crying hopelessly at nights. I contemplated the option of suicide with growing seriousness..."

Sir Ranulph Fiennes, explorer

Discussion - The battleground

It was Rutter[1] who noted in 1979 that children spend 15,000 hours in secondary school and he showed that even in disadvantaged areas, the 'ethos' of the school could separate out those children who thrived from those who did not. For young people who are bullied, secondary school can mean up to 15,000 hours of possible torment.

Australian family therapist and author, Steve Biddulph[2] points out how schools play a big part both in creating the problem of bullying – and in curing it. Less able students, for example, belittled in the competitive atmosphere, may strive to regain some dignity through bullying. When helped to learn in a dignified way they can change. Many teachers bully their students or tacitly permit the singling out of an individual, even ridiculing someone in front of the others. Biddulph points out that school sport has the potential for learning team spirit,

shared endeavour, giving your best and loyalty. But it can exclude those who don't excel. It can become brutish and be influenced by professional sport with excesses such as over-competitiveness, binge drinking, over stressing the body and violence. Sports injuries from rugby, cricket, football and baseball are common. Sports kit is regularly being used as a weapon in bullying.

Boarding school in particular has these possibilities writ large, as Sir Ranulph Fiennes[3], one of the world's greatest living explorers describes above. Bullying knows no boundaries and triumphs equally in schools that are disadvantaged or luxurious. It can also be reduced in all settings.

Policies only in glossy brochures

Too many schools have impressive anti-bullying statements only in their prospectus. They may even have a strategy document in a filing cabinet. Too few are implementing it

actively and re-negotiating as necessary. It should be acknowledged that it is a very difficult undertaking to get it up and running fully.

For 15 months, the extensive Sheffield project[4] undertook various interventions in 23 schools in Britain. The studies, undertaken by Smith and Sharp, considered which interventions worked. Through anonymous polling of pupils, they were able to measure their effectiveness. This valuable work concluded that an anti-bullying strategy to be effective, must involve the whole school community down to caretakers, dinner ladies and indeed teachers, pupils and parents. This information with details of types of intervention was made available to schools[5], but 2772 young people polled anew by Young Voice in 2000[6], report that a considerable number of schools still do not have an anti-bullying strategy – despite being required to do so since September 1999[7].

Three quarters unprotected

The results show that in March 2000,

■ 43% of girls and 45% of boys say their school still does not have such a policy.

■ Of those who said their school does have a policy, no more than 49% of girls and 54% of boys thought it was working.

Our anonymous surveys have asked this question three times, in 1996, 1998 and 2000. This involved a total of over 7000 young people. Three quarters of the young people still say that their school does not have an effective anti-bullying policy that works. While some schools are to be applauded for their innovative and vigorous efforts, too many are ignoring the problem. Some have interventions but they are not effective.

The effect can fade

Even where there has been a lot of dedicated work on bullying, the effect may fade with time or as staff change. In studies in the UK and elsewhere, in roughly between 50% and 80% of schools where an intervention programme had been based, bullying levels were found to drift upwards to original levels after three or five year periods[8].

rising. The Norwegian studies suggest that bullying is on the increase, paralleled by an increase in violent crime which has gone up 900% since the '60's.

Why implement a strategy?

When a programme is implemented in Primary schools, there has been a definite reduction in bullying, of up to 55%. At ages 13/14, clear effects on anti-social behaviour, vandalism, theft, truancy, and classroom climate, plus attitudes to school and teachers, have been noted by Olweus when his anti-bullying programme[10] is active. 60% of former bullies are likely to have a conviction by the age of 24 - reason enough for society to want to reduce bullying. Academic standards are raised when bullying is reduced and the social ethos is improved[11].

Having looked at school bullying from the evidence and perspective of researchers, what did we learn from young people in Britain? Below we hear from them.

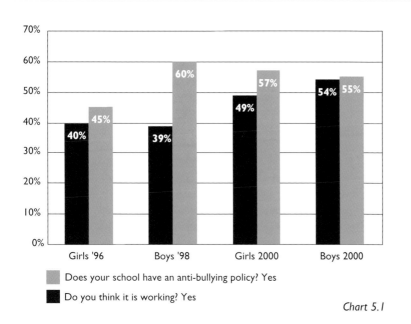

School anti-bullying policies. Three surveys

Chart data:
- Girls '96: Does your school have an anti-bullying policy? Yes 45%; Do you think it is working? Yes 40%
- Boys '98: policy 60%; working 39%
- Girls 2000: policy 57%; working 49%
- Boys 2000: policy 55%; working 54%

Legend:
- Does your school have an anti-bullying policy? Yes
- Do you think it is working? Yes

Chart 5.1

Resistance from staff

There may be resistance or suspicion from teachers and heads to get involved in an anti bullying strategy. Indeed for this report a number of heads said "We have no bullying here, we don't need a policy" or "if you make a big thing of a policy, parents will think you have a bullying problem in your school". Some teachers bully others in the staffroom and resist a whole school ethos change. They may believe children should stand up for themselves.

Olweus[9] also describes 'drift' a withering away of the effectiveness of a policy over three years, which he found in the monitoring of schools in Norway.

Keeping an anti-bullying policy alive and well, involves re-invigorating it, inducting each new intake and involving everyone anew. An active policy may induce higher reporting rates at first which could give the impression that bullying is

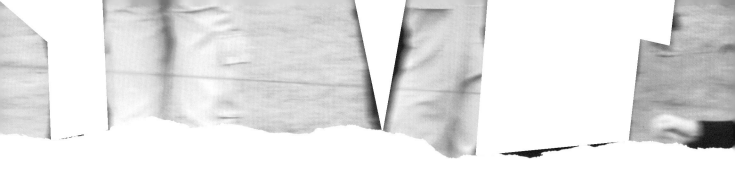

THE BULLIED

Attitudes to school

Young people's feelings about school, their work and teachers were strongly linked with their experiences of bullying. This is expected. What is interesting is how males and females reacted. Boys tended to become anti-school while bullied girls buried themselves in school work. Over 30% of the severely bullied boys were 'anti-school'[12] whereas only 14% of those who weren't bullied felt the same. 14% of severely bullied boys said they 'never took their work seriously' compared to only 4% of their non bullied peers. Tellingly bullied boys were more likely to say that their 'teachers made them feel stupid if they made a mistake' and that 'teachers did not know me as a person'.

The picture they describe, is one of powerlessness, they are indeed effaced. The apparently negative attitudes seen amongst the bullied boys seemed to hide the fact that both bullied boys and girls were often overwhelmed by worries about their work. The two gender groups reacted in different ways to their situation with bullied girls more likely to say that they 'just get on with my work'. The quieter people, seemingly working calmly, may go unnoticed by the teacher as they are not 'making waves'. However this may conceal deep social difficulties.

"If you get a good mark and people say you're a boff, just laugh it off don't let it be a big thing – keep it a joke"

Girl 13 London

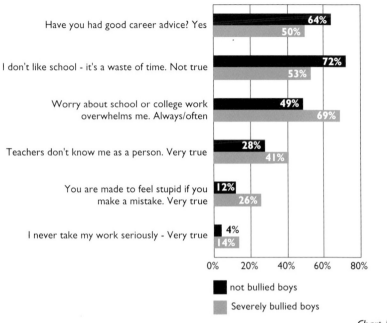

Bullied boys' views about school and teachers

Have you had good career advice? Yes — 64% / 50%

I don't like school - it's a waste of time. Not true — 72% / 53%

Worry about school or college work overwhelms me. Always/often — 49% / 69%

Teachers don't know me as a person. Very true — 28% / 41%

You are made to feel stupid if you make a mistake. Very true — 12% / 26%

I never take my work seriously - Very true — 4% / 14%

■ not bullied boys
■ Severely bullied boys

Chart 5.2

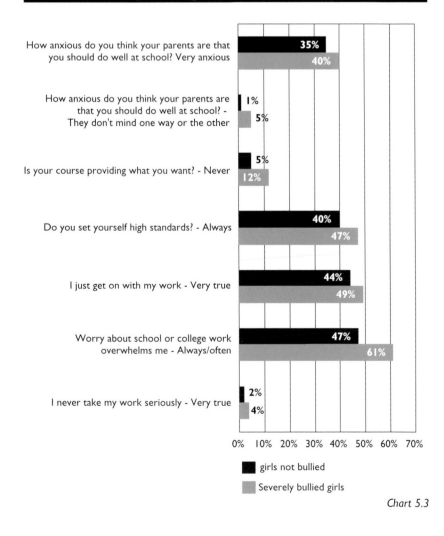

Severely bullied girls and attitudes to school

How anxious do you think your parents are that you should do well at school? Very anxious — 35% / 40%

How anxious do you think your parents are that you should do well at school? - They don't mind one way or the other — 1% / 5%

Is your course providing what you want? - Never — 5% / 12%

Do you set yourself high standards? - Always — 40% / 47%

I just get on with my work - Very true — 44% / 49%

Worry about school or college work overwhelms me - Always/often — 47% / 61%

I never take my work seriously - Very true — 2% / 4%

■ girls not bullied
■ Severely bullied girls

Chart 5.3

As shown in chart 5.3, bullied girls appear more likely to have parents who are a little more anxious than average about their schoolwork, or conversely in the case of a few, do not care one way or the other. These girls are more likely to feel overwhelmed by worries about work, and set themselves high standards more often than none bullied girls. It may be useful to praise such a girl in private but not keep singling her out in front of the others. She may be bullied more as she appears to be a teachers' pet.

In line with recent results in both GCSE and A levels, and perhaps as a response to the culture of girls' academic success, over 85% of all girls whether bullied or not, emphatically disagreed with the statement 'I cannot see the point of studying'. However more positive attitudes to school generally were found among those who had not been bullied.

The anti-swot culture

There is a pervasive anti-swot culture. Just under one third of male bullies and non-bullies said it was 'very true' that 'I don't want to appear a swot'.

This sentiment was echoed exactly by the severely bullied boys. A further 41% of bullies said this statement was 'partly true', as did around a third of victims.

In the March 2000 survey, 20% of sixteen year olds said that they had been bullied because they were good at schoolwork.

Usefulness and delivery of their course and careers advice

Severely bullied girls were more likely to say that the course "never provided what they wanted", than girls who weren't bullied. (12% vs 5%) Both male and female victims are more likely to feel that their course was 'never' delivered well. Boys in particular felt this way: 18% of severely bullied boys in contrast to 8% of boys who weren't bullied.

Home/school pressures

Young people were asked about their parents showing interest in schoolwork and putting on pressure. Thus anxiety interest and pressure were separated out. Young people who were bullied, frequently experienced further stress, as they were also under pressure about their work from home. Boys and girls who'd been severely bullied, tended to feel that both parents and teachers were putting on too much pressure. Bullied girls were very significantly more likely to say that the interest parents take in them, is 'rarely or never about right'. On the other hand they were very significantly more likely to say that parents always put too much pressure on them.

> **"I was bullied by the same people for over a year. It was mean and I was beaten up. The school did nothing to help although we told them. It got absolutely desperate until it was either my life or change school. Eventually I changed school and got my life back."**
>
> Male 16 Suffolk

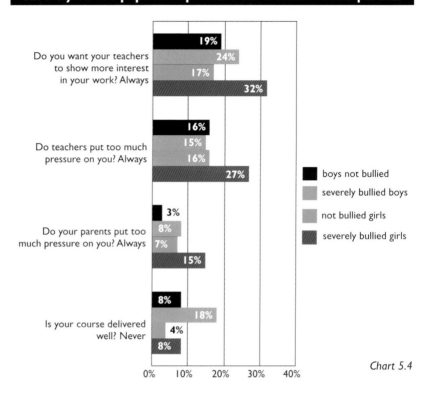

Severely bullied pupils and pressure from teachers and parents

Do you want your teachers to show more interest in your work? Always
- 19%
- 24%
- 17%
- 32%

Do teachers put too much pressure on you? Always
- 16%
- 15%
- 16%
- 27%

Do your parents put too much pressure on you? Always
- 3%
- 8%
- 7%
- 15%

Is your course delivered well? Never
- 8%
- 18%
- 4%
- 8%

Legend:
- ■ boys not bullied
- severely bullied boys
- not bullied girls
- severely bullied girls

0% 10% 20% 30% 40%

Chart 5.4

Here, as in other parts of the study, we only know one side of the story – the young people's perspective. We also have no independent measure of how the young people were doing at school or their level of ability. We do not know whether bullying is leading to a lower level of achievement in school or whether a higher or lower level of achievement is leading to the bullying. Either way, a sense of failure and worry is piling up on these children. Sadly, nearly a third of the severely bullied girls wanted the teachers to show more interest in their work. They may be the quiet ones, getting little attention because they don't make trouble.

Anti-bullying policies

Anti-bullying policies are central to prevent bullying. But the young people surveyed for this study confirmed that it was not good enough just to have a policy, it has to be working (page 35).

There was considerable agreement amongst over three quarters of the bullied children that it was not

working. 57% of bullied boys and 64% of bullied girls said their schools did have a policy. But 78% and 84% respectively said these policies in place in their schools didn't work.

> **"It's got better for me, I got more confident. I'm still short, but when picked on I fought back. You have to. It's a chance you have to take. If you all got together and faced the bully...some people are scared. I was scared and sometimes if you tell, it gets worse. I faced them me self. If he gets respect off his mates it'll go on. You have to teach people, but it would take time to change things. I'd tell a younger boy: Make sure they don't see you as a pushover, and respect ya for having a go back. They get a buzz off doing this.(making you scared) I'd tell a kid to see me or face it. Don't let 'em take advantage and the bigger they are the harder they fall."**
>
> 21 Male prisoner

THE BULLIES

Clearly school is an unhappy environment for bullied children, but it was not necessarily a happy place for bullies either. Although proportionately fewer bullies than victims were 'anti-school', one in five of the male bullies disliked it and around one in ten 'never take their work seriously'. Like the victims, the male bullies were worried about 'being made to feel stupid if they made a mistake', and more than half often feel overwhelmed by anxiety about their work

A similar pattern emerged with other attitudes to school. Bullies were more inclined to say school is 'a waste of time'. They were also less likely to say that they 'just got on with their work'.

Usefulness and delivery of their course and careers advice

Girl bullies were more negative in their attitudes about their course and its delivery, as well as the careers advice they had been given. Bullies of both sexes were also more likely than the non-bullies to feel their course had never been delivered well.

> ## "One of my teachers told me she doesn't like teaching in a single sex boys school. So you wouldn't go to her would you."
>
> Male 16 Hartleypool

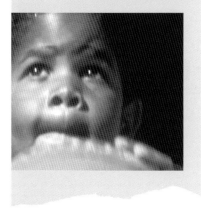

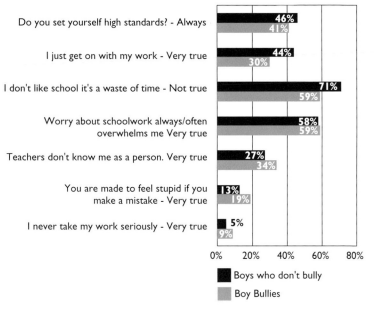

Boys who bully and attitudes to school

	Boys who don't bully	Boy Bullies
Do you set yourself high standards? - Always	46%	41%
I just get on with my work - Very true	44%	30%
I don't like school it's a waste of time - Not true	71%	59%
Worry about schoolwork always/often overwhelms me Very true	58%	59%
Teachers don't know me as a person. Very true	27%	34%
You are made to feel stupid if you make a mistake - Very true	13%	19%
I never take my work seriously - Very true	5%	9%

■ Boys who don't bully

■ Boy Bullies

Chart 5.5

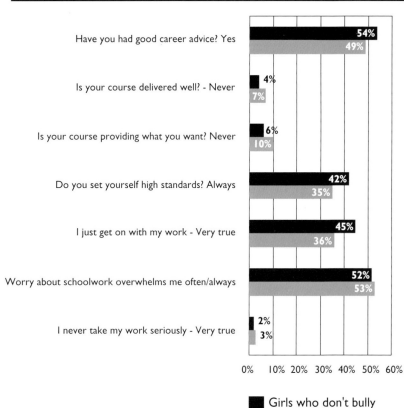

Girls who bully and attitudes to school

Have you had good career advice? Yes — 54% / 49%

Is your course delivered well? - Never — 4% / 7%

Is your course providing what you want? Never — 6% / 10%

Do you set yourself high standards? Always — 42% / 35%

I just get on with my work - Very true — 45% / 36%

Worry about schoolwork overwhelms me often/always — 52% / 53%

I never take my work seriously - Very true — 2% / 3%

0% 10% 20% 30% 40% 50% 60%

■ Girls who don't bully
■ Girls who bully

Chart 5.6

Home school pressures

Like the targets, the bullies themselves were also under more pressure from home than young people who did not bully. In addition, the male bullies were likely to feel the pressure from teachers was too much.

Anti bullying policies

In common with the bullied students, a very similar proportion of the bullies felt their school had an anti-bullying policy. The key difference between those who were bullies and those who weren't, was not whether their school had an anti-bullying policy, but whether the young people felt it was working. Girl bullies were the most likely group to say a policy wasn't working. Girls' subtle nastiness may be the hardest to detect and deal with.

"I'd like to see the bullies being stopped from bullying. There should be security at bus stations, the bus drivers can throw 'em off. They should teach how to stand up to them then the bully would back off."

Male prisoner 18

"If you can't help someone else, how 're you gonna help yourself? You have to ask yourself, what would they do if you were getting bullied? If they would help, why aren't you? Children didn't think about what would happen if it was you. But people are starting to realise this. It is getting into classes more and more. Teachers don't encourage laughing at someone else. In my old school we did have a couple of talks when someone came down and told us if you gang up on the bully he can't get away with it. But straight after people are bullied, they can't believe it'll get better."

Male 13 Herts

"It's got worse, there's more of it, I know it's more. If he were getting bullied I'd tell him to tell the teacher – it's worth a try."

21 Male on remand

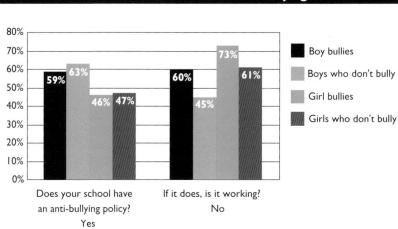

Bullies' views on school anti-bullying

Does your school have an anti-bullying policy? Yes — 59% / 63% / 46% / 47%

If it does, is it working? No — 60% / 45% / 73% / 61%

■ Boy bullies
■ Boys who don't bully
■ Girl bullies
▨ Girls who don't bully

Chart 5.7

Summary

■ Young people who were severely bullied had, as might be expected, fairly negative attitudes to school, their teachers and to work.

■ Some girls who were severely bullied took refuge in their work. They tended to set themselves high standards and just get on with their work, but wanted teachers to show more interest in them without applying pressure. They were often overwhelmed with worry about work.

■ The bullies too, were less happy at school than pupils who didn't bully others. They reflected negative attitudes to school, work and their teachers.

■ Both the bullied and the bullies were more inclined to be negative about the way their course was delivered, its usefulness and the careers advice they had been given.

■ Similarly the bullied and the bullies were more likely than those who were neither bully nor target, to feel under pressure from their parents and teachers about their work. (Particularly girls).

■ Regarding school anti-bullying policies - the key difference in the case of people experiencing or inflicting bullying, was not whether they had such a policy in their school but whether in their view the policy was working.

■ Too few schools were implementing a policy at all (a little over a half) and of these, well under half were thought to be working effectively. There was however some increase in the number of people who said their school had a policy, between the girls' survey of 1996 (45%) and the boys' undertaken in 1998 (60%).

■ By 2000 when a new survey was taken 55% of boys and girls said their school had a policy in place, of these only half thought it was working.

ADVICE

"I'd say don't draw attention to yourself – integrate don't make people jealous of you – fit in easily and be down to earth. It's not advisable to pull yourself back to fit in with the rest if you're higher academically. First impressions really matter – get people on your side the worst thing is for teachers to start photocopying your work and showing it to people. Now the teachers will call you up to him and talk to you – not give out work and marks in front of everyone. Lower in the school they won't read out marks – just hand out which keeps privacy. Positions in class work quite detrimentally – coming last does you no good at all."

Prefect doing peer support training

"The new head's only been here a short time but he's laying down rules. I hear it's got a lot better. In our (primary) school the head wanted to be convinced there wasn't any bullying, she said it was teasing and she didn't want to admit it. One boy was always teased and sworn at all the time so he had to leave. There's no nicking of kit. There's swearing and annoying you."

Male 13 Herts

"My form tutor in PSE lessons makes clear that bullying is not accepted here. This shows that something will be done about it. Our tutor was saying that you can come and talk to me - I'll do what you want. She'll ask others to be supportive to a girl and talk to her really quietly - she can help."

Girl 13

"There are prefects, but people don't know them really. There are loads of rumours about older pupils meeting other people from other schools and beating people up with belts and mugging."

Girl 13 Essex

"That's why bullying is so horrible because you can't stop someone from bullying someone else its just impossible."

Girl 18

[1] Rutter, M. Maughan, B. Mortimore, P. and Ouston, J. 1979 "Fifteen thousand hours: Secondary schools and their effects on children. London. Open Books.

[2] Biddulph, Steve, Raising Boys, Thorsons UK 1998

[3] Quoted by Kidscape and here with permission from Sir Ranulph,.

[4] The DES Sheffield Bullying Project 1993 Dept of Psychology University of Sheffield. Smith PK and Sharp, S. eds (1994) School Bullying: Insights and perspectives. Routledge

[5] 'Don't Suffer in silence'. An Anti-Bullying pack for schools. DfEE 1994, HMSO

[6] Data collection was made possible by Sky TV.

[7] Section 61(4)(B) of the School Standards & Framework Act, 1998

[8] Thompson, D 'Problems in Maintaining school anti-bullying policies'. University of Sheffield, School of Education.

[9] Olweus, D. as above, speaking at A.C.P.P. conference 'Bullying In Schools' November 2000

[10] Olweus' Core Program against Bullying and Anti-social behaviour' was selected to be used in a national violence prevention initiative in the USA (1999-2002) supported by the US dept of Justice. Olweus & Limber 1999.

[11] Lynn Ackland and Durham LEA anti bullying programme.

[12] Criteria for being categorized 'anti-school' can be found on page 73

 "The widespread and systematic failure to meaningfully assess a persons' past experience of violence or tragedy and to ignore the impact of this, is the psychological equivalent of failing to ask a patient with breathing difficulties if they smoke…Ignoring the direct links between the experience of violence in all its many forms and personal distress, is nothing short of a modern tragedy." [1]

A striking finding in this study was the link between bullying and violence encountered beyond the bullying arena. Both bullies and victims revealed experiences of physical punishment and violence in the home and elsewhere in their lives.

THE BULLIED

Violence in the home

Those who were bullied tended to have been smacked or beaten more often. They were more likely to say they had experienced an adult using violence against them.

By asking separate questions in the survey about smacking, hitting and beating, it was clear that different levels of physical punishment were being assessed. Young people could reply separately to each of these questions.

Compared to those who were not bullied - the findings are stark:

■ More than a third of the severely bullied boys had been beaten and more than 40% had experienced an adult using violence against them, compared to 7% and 11% respectively for boys who weren't bullied.

Although fewer girls experienced violence, the differences between those girls who were bullied and those who were not, were highly significant:

■ 31% percent, of the severely bullied girls, had experienced an adult using violence against them in contrast to 11% of girls who weren't bullied.

■ Although beating girls is relatively rare, bullied girls were more than four times as likely as non-bullied girls to say they had been beaten.

Girls who were targeted by bullies were also twice as likely to have experienced violent threats from an adult. Bullied children of both sexes reported arguing more often with parents.

The consequences of this on their sense of self may be imagined. Do they come to see themselves as deserving punishment? Are they conditioned to be victims? These questions cannot be answered in this study, but the links found here between the widespread experience of violence these bullied children report, and the fact that they are also the victims of severe bullying, provides an area for future investigation.

These findings also raise the need to consider and put in place, wider support for victims of bullying. This is hinted at by ChildLine in notes on Helping Children to Recover, in a book titled 'Why Me?'[2] where findings from a bullying helpline are discussed. 'Alongside action to put a stop to the bullying, must go attention to the child's emotional state. The children ringing ChildLine are eloquent in describing the level of fear, disablement and anguish they experience. Children involved in bullying, whether bullied, bystanders or bullies, may need ongoing help for some period of time to resolve the emotional impact of bullying and/or difficulties within the family, school or the individual.'

(Note in the charts below, responses were slightly different for boys and girls. Boys' replies were A little/ a lot and have been shown as Yes, Girls' replies were often/sometimes and are shown as Yes.)

Willingness to use violence

Different patterns emerged when boys and girls were compared on the question of whether they would be prepared to use violence to defend themselves. More than eight out of ten boys who were not bullied said they would defend themselves using violence if necessary, but distinctly fewer bullied boys were willing to use violence in self defence. Among girls the opposite was found. Rather more bullied girls were willing to use violence to defend themselves than non-bullied girls.

When it came to using violence to defend another – this pattern was repeated. Boys who weren't bullied were more likely to say they'd use violence to defend someone else than severely bullied boys. The picture for girls was dramatically different however. 61% of severely bullied girls compared to 49% of non-bullied girls would use violence to defend someone else.

Severely bullied boys and experiences of violence beyond bullying

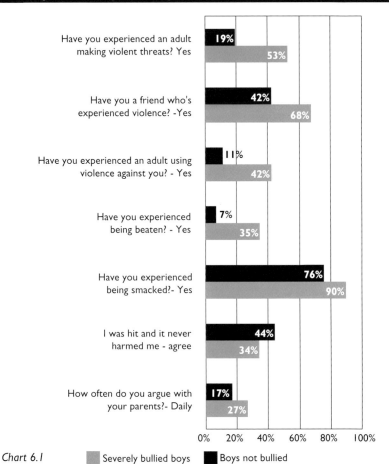

Have you experienced an adult making violent threats? Yes — 19% / 53%

Have you a friend who's experienced violence? -Yes — 42% / 68%

Have you experienced an adult using violence against you? - Yes — 11% / 42%

Have you experienced being beaten? - Yes — 7% / 35%

Have you experienced being smacked?- Yes — 76% / 90%

I was hit and it never harmed me - agree — 44% / 34%

How often do you argue with your parents?- Daily — 17% / 27%

0% 20% 40% 60% 80% 100%

Chart 6.1 ▓ Severely bullied boys ■ Boys not bullied

"People are getting more violent – they snap quicker these days. Younger people are learning things too fast. I don't think you'll ever stop the violence, people are getting guns now, no one's too small to carry a trigger. They're watching films. It's like America, All they doing now is sitting at home watching telly or computers. They should say there 's no need for you to prove your strength. I've seen people take a brick and smash his head - it's just a circle isn't it? A vicious circle. I can't stand bullies meself, they intimidate people – it's not the same as a fight. They get a buzz off it if a person shows fear."

Male 21 prisoner

Severely bullied girls and experiences of violence beyond bullying

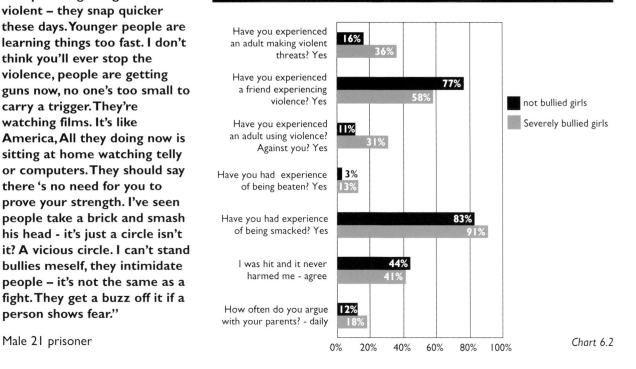

Have you experienced an adult making violent threats? Yes — 16% / 36%

Have you experienced a friend experiencing violence? Yes — 77% / 58%

Have you experienced an adult using violence? Against you? Yes — 11% / 31%

Have you had experience of being beaten? Yes — 3% / 13%

Have you had experience of being smacked? Yes — 83% / 91%

I was hit and it never harmed me - agree — 44% / 41%

How often do you argue with your parents? - daily — 12% / 18%

■ not bullied girls ▓ Severely bullied girls

0% 20% 40% 60% 80% 100%

Chart 6.2

43

Of concern was the greater willingness of the bullied children both male and female, to say it was OK to use violence to get what you wanted. The bullied boys were also significantly more likely to feel it was OK to use violence to discipline a child. In this way the cycle of violence may be perpetuated.

An interesting debate was had within several interviews. When asked what they thought should happen to bullies, people whose parents used physical or harsh punishment, tended to suggest bullies were given increasingly more physical punishment. When asked whether they thought this would work, a number said 'No'. But they believed that punishment of this sort was the only option available. They also felt that the victim would feel satisfaction.

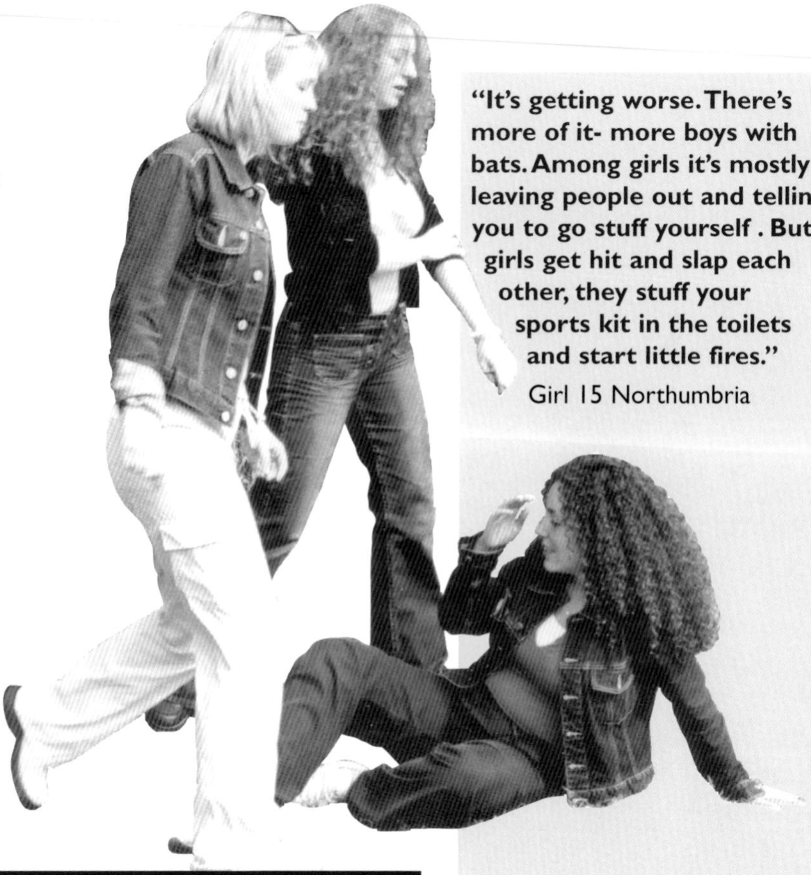

"It's getting worse. There's more of it- more boys with bats. Among girls it's mostly leaving people out and telling you to go stuff yourself . But girls get hit and slap each other, they stuff your sports kit in the toilets and start little fires."

Girl 15 Northumbria

Bullied boys' attitudes to violence

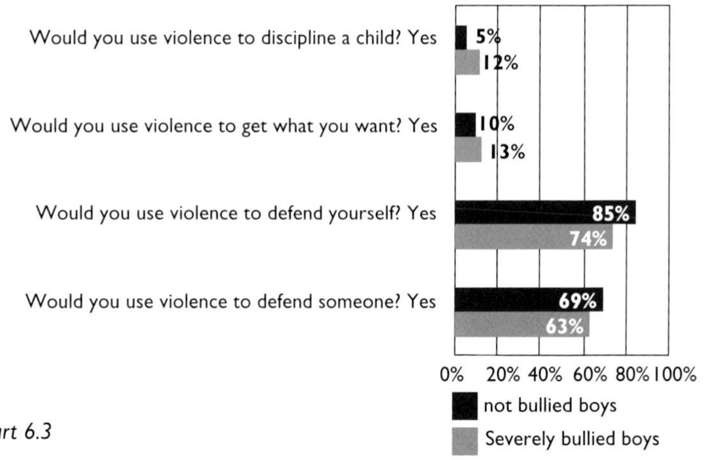

Would you use violence to discipline a child? Yes	5% / 12%
Would you use violence to get what you want? Yes	10% / 13%
Would you use violence to defend yourself? Yes	85% / 74%
Would you use violence to defend someone? Yes	69% / 63%

0% 20% 40% 60% 80% 100%

■ not bullied boys
■ Severely bullied boys

Chart 6.3

"I'd say to her not to take shit off people – they hate you – you gotta hate them. It'll probably get worse even become a fight but you gotta be like that. Don't give them anything they want don't keep saying 'yes' cos then they'll push you into something. They could take clothes off you, don't wear new stuff clothes and trainers."

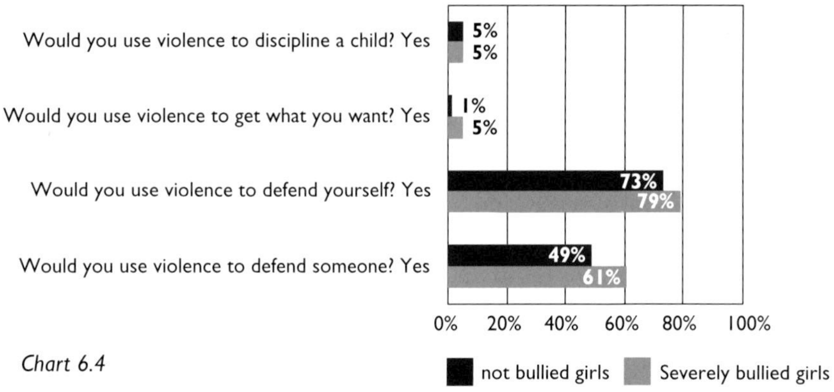

Girl 13 Northumbria

"There's a lot of bullying both violent and fights. Girls are slapping and shouting. They set this fire and boys pushed coats down the loos. You have no lockers you have to carry your books and games kit all day. If you leave it on the porch it gets taken."

Girl 12 Northumbria

Bullied girls' attitudes to violence

Would you use violence to discipline a child? Yes	5% / 5%
Would you use violence to get what you want? Yes	1% / 5%
Would you use violence to defend yourself? Yes	73% / 79%
Would you use violence to defend someone? Yes	49% / 61%

0% 20% 40% 60% 80% 100%

■ not bullied girls ■ Severely bullied girls

Chart 6.4

THE BULLIES

 Violence in the background was not confined to the people who had been bullied. Significantly more of the bullies had been physically punished and had experienced other forms of violence in their lives than young people who did not bully. It is as though bullies and victims have a common experience of seeing or living through higher levels violence, than other children. However, although violence was more commonly a factor in the lives of both bullies and victims, that does not tell us that all bullies and all victims experienced it.

Girls who bully are strikingly more likely to say they have a friend who has experienced violence. (58% vs 42% of non-bullies). Compounding the picture, well over a quarter of them have personally experienced violence from an adult. They are almost twice as likely to report that they have been beaten. (Chart 6.6)

Bullies of both sexes are more likely to argue with their parents 'daily' than children who don't bully, and male bullies are more likely to say their parents 'fight a lot with each other'.

■ Almost one in five male bullies has been beaten and one third has experienced an adult using violence against him.

Despite the strong message from these findings on violence in the lives of the bullies it is noticeable that the bullied young people report even higher levels of violence experienced personally. As we saw on page 43, 35% of bullied males said they had been beaten, while 19% of male bullies reported this. This pattern was also seen among girls: 13% of bullied girls had been beaten compared to 9% of girl bullies. Yet both these bullies and their targets were more likely to have encountered beating than non victims or non bullies.

31% of the bullied females had experienced an adult using violence against her, a particularly high figure yet girl bullies were close behind with 28% of them reporting the same experience.

Male bullies and experience

Have you experienced a friend experiencing violence? Yes
- **47%** (Boys who don't bully)
- 64% (Boy bullies)

Have you experienced an adult using violence aagainst you? Yes
- **27%** (Boys who don't bully)
- 33% (Boy bullies)

Have you experienced being beaten? Yes
- **12%** (Boys who don't bully)
- 19% (Boy bullies)

Have you experienced being smacked? Yes
- **82%** (Boys who don't bully)
- 89% (Boy bullies)

I was hit and it never harmed me. Agree
- **41%** (Boys who don't bully)
- 47% (Boy bullies)

How often do you argue with your parents? Daily
- **15%** (Boys who don't bully)
- 23% (Boy bullies)

My parents fight a lot with each other Yes
- **8%** (Boys who don't bully)
- 12% (Boy bullies)

0% 20% 40% 60% 80% 100%

■ Boys who don't bully
■ Boy bullies

Chart 6.5

Girl bullies and their experience of violence

Have you experienced a friend experiencing violence? Yes
- **42%** (Girls who don't bully)
- 58% (Girl bullies)

Have you experienced an adult using violence against you? Yes
- **15%** (Girls who don't bully)
- 28% (Girl bullies)

Have you experienced being beaten? Yes
- **5%** (Girls who don't bully)
- 9% (Girl bullies)

Have you experienced being smacked? Yes
- **12%** (Girls who don't bully)
- 16% (Girl bullies)

I was hit and it never harmed me - agree
- **43%** (Girls who don't bully)
- 47% (Girl bullies)

How often do you argue with your parents? Daily
- **12%** (Girls who don't bully)
- 18% (Girl bullies)

0% 10% 20% 30% 40% 50% 60% 70%

■ Girls who don't bully
■ Girl bullies

Chart 6.6

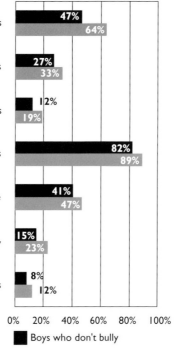

> **"I was a member of a gang, in a way it was comforting. It was an all boy gang, some would help you if you were in trouble. There were older and younger boys in it."**
>
> Boy 18 London

Bullying causes ripples

Bullying is a vital social indicator. There is the immediate need to make children safe. But there are other ripples from bullying that have an effect within society long after the bullying takes place. Research has found that bullies more frequently go on to have a criminal record by the time they are twenty four, than young men who don't bully.[3] In a small sub group of young men on remand who agreed to answer questions on bullying for this study, it was noticeable that ten out of sixteen admitted they had been bullies and six had experienced violence from an adult. Half of them believed that the best way to deal with bullying was to fight back physically and half said it was to tell someone. (They have come into contact with an anti-bullying policy within the prison). Eleven of them would smash things up when they became distressed.[4]

■ Willingness to use violence

Like young people who were bullied, the bullies were more willing to use violence. Three times as many boy and girl bullies were prepared to use violence to get what they wanted than non-bullies. The bullies were also more prepared to use violence to defend someone (particularly girl bullies) they would use violence to defend themselves, and the male bullies were significantly more prepared to use violence to discipline a child.

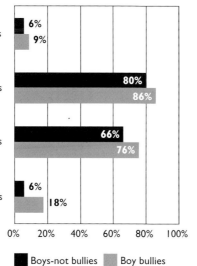

Boy bullies and attitudes to violence

Would you use violence to discipline a child? Yes
- 6%
- 9%

Would you use violence to defend yourself? Yes
- 80%
- 86%

Would you use violence to defend someone? Yes
- 66%
- 76%

Would you use violence to get what you want? Yes
- 6%
- 18%

0% 20% 40% 60% 80% 100%

■ Boys-not bullies ■ Boy bullies

Chart 6.7

Girl bullies and attitudes to violence

Would you use violence to discipline a child? Yes
- 5%
- 6%

Would you use violence to defend yourself? Yes
- 73%
- 81%

Would you use violence to defend someone? Yes
- 51%
- 64%

Would you use violence to get what you want? Yes
- 1%
- 4%

0% 20% 40% 60% 80% 100%

■ Girls who don't bully ■ Bully girls

Chart 6.8

The pressure on teenagers to belong to a group almost certainly means defining your group as distinct from other people, who by definition will be left out. Secondary school pupils are under enormous social strain as they struggle for acceptance, and many will look to peer leaders and the school itself to set a tone – create an atmosphere to which they will conform.

Children are not saints despite the idealized vision of childhood often put forward. They, like any other person, will sometimes act unreasonably or enjoy being nasty or bitchy to someone. Like adults they might enjoy having power over another. But if they are encouraged to act repeatedly in this way by peers, circumstances at home and the ethos at school, this can escalate dangerously out of control. A few have not developed a strong sense of conscience or trust in others at a young age and have little sense of wrongdoing. The responsibility lies with adults to protect and teach future citizens to deal with one another reasonably in a culture of respect and decency. This chapter has shown that some adults are instead providing a message that violence is power.

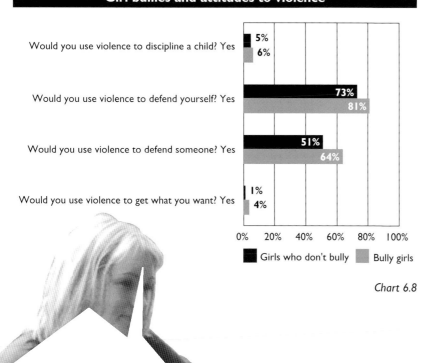

Questions for classroom debate:

Does punishing the bully help? Or does it demonstrate a bullying style of punishment and perpetuate the problem? What other methods could be used so that children see that the bully does not seem to get away with it? What other skills could we learn that would help us get on better? How can you resolve conflict without aggression? Is violence always wrong? Should you defend yourself by fighting back?

'Non-punitive approaches like the no-blame approach, allow children to change their behaviour without feeling so bad about themselves that they have even more bad feelings to take out on others.' Childline

'Children ringing ChildLine tell us that adults, teachers and parents bully too.'

Other suggestions from this Young Voice study are: 'It's mainly jealousy. It's the sort of person who always puts their hand up, always knows everything that gets it. Its like this girl who's really rich – at first people couldn't take her – now she's calmed down a bit. She's learned – don't rub it in.'

"I was small and mouthy I suppose, so I got bullied."
Boy 16

"I made a friend and then one day he started hitting me he called me gay and stuff. Three of his mates started pushing me, this lad kicked me in the leg and slammed my head against the window then they started pushing me into the English teacher every time."
Male year 9 Liverpool

"You might be tempted to say I'll beat him up for you, but I think she should talk to people and not keep it to herself or get into a major fight. Ignoring it can work it depends what the bullying is."
Girl 13 Essex

Summary

■ A key difference between those caught up in bullying, either as perpetrator or victim, when compared to other children, was the extent to which they had been physically punished, and experienced or witnessed violence in the home. For many of the bullied children and the bullies - violence of one form or another was an everyday reality.

■ Children who had been bullied reported experiencing a higher level of violence than bullies although both groups reported higher levels than non bullies and those who were not bullied.

■ The second key difference was the willingness of both the bullied and the bullies to use violence to sort out their concerns.

"Loads of lads just fight after school. Once the teacher got hit trying to separate them. If it goes on you should be punished more severely – they should punish the bully more."

Male 16 Liverpool

"My brother keeps coming home and saying there's a boy in the class above him who keeps hitting him. I just say fight back!"

Girl 15 Twickenham

"I think bullying is getting worse, they've got knives now it's more dangerous. There are gangs, it's out of school mostly at big bus stops with gangs of kids at every corner. Kids from other estates. When I was younger there wasn't so much trouble here. There should be more police and people in cars. No one does anything. People are scared and can't help. I don't know what does help – really. I've never seen a programme that works. Society isn't protecting children. I've been bullied – it stays with you. Now its drugs, people want drugs and they want money. People get threatened with knives – schools just give up. I'd talk to a child to try and like, make him protect himself and come and tell us. If I were a father I'd say to a kid – come and talk to me."

Male 17 Newcastle

"There is bullying in school, people took dinner money, hats and trainers all the time. There are loads of police on the streets it don't make no difference. There should be more activities for young people. People are bored they've got nowt to do. They should have youth clubs and sport."

Male 16 Newcastle

"It's getting worse there's more of it and its more violent. Schools reduce bullying and it goes outside. I'd say if anyone hits you – hit them back. Tell the teacher. It's usually people from other estates. Most of my friends I've had since primary school, we went on to secondary together. So we know each other really well and there's no bullying among us. There should be more schemes and awards to stop it. Training to sort out anger. They should do something about violence in general. Like stricter laws. They should say its not gonna be tolerated. It was stopped by my old school."

Male 16 Newcastle

"Our school is next door to two others - there were loads of hostilities between them and our school. People punched at the bus stop for no reason and that. But the heads are trying to change things. Joining us in music, drama and sport. We have a new head who is strict on these issues."

Male 17 Middlesex

"Year 7 and 8 are vicious. If bad words are said a group goes round and fights. Youth clubs make a difference, people from other schools meet each other there and get to know them. A person who is bullied is affected always. Would I intervene? If you're bigger you can."

15 Twickenham

[1] Godsi, E. 1999 'Making sense: towards a social ecology' in Violence in Society', Constable, London

[2] MacLeod, M. Morris, S. (1996) Why Me? ChildLine London

[3] Olweus, D. 1973 60% of former bullies had a conviction at age 24

[4] We are grateful to Anne Renton of The New Bridge project for her help in having these questionnaires completed.

"It's just wrong to treat someone like that."

Girl 14 Cardiff

THE BULLIED

Views about right and wrong

Religion

Nearly all young people had strong views about right and wrong. Where did these views come from? Few chose to say that these views were influenced by their religion, except for bullied boys, which suggests they are being bullied for their religion.

Parents

Most young people felt their views on right and wrong were the same as their parents but this was less likely to be true for severely bullied girls and boys. This is interesting because research has suggested that bullied children are frequently closely enmeshed with their families in an almost overprotective embrace[1].

In Chapter Two we saw that compared to those children who weren't bullied, severely bullied boys

"We wear ripped jeans, they are the booted suited mob. They hate us."
Male 14

and girls were far more likely to describe their parents as trying to 'control everything I do', or 'treat me like a baby'. But they were also more likely to say that their parents 'take no notice of me'.

In chapter six a considerable number of severely bullied children experience beatings and adult violence. It is not surprising then - after finding that bullied children report a diverse range of parenting

behaviours that differ from the majority - to see that over a third of bullied girls and boys hold different values from their parents. This is a reminder of the complexity of this picture. Bullied children may come to feel isolated in many ways. These perceptions from the children are self reported on one particular day and may of course reflect how they felt at the time of the survey.

Friends

This severely bullied group differed in another way too. Whilst most young people felt their views on right and wrong were the same as those of their friends – the badly bullied children were far less likely to say so. When tested these figures were very significant. Are they being bullied because they won't do what the others are pressuring them to do? We cannot tell from the survey data but in face to face interviews we heard time and again that if people 'did not fit in' they were likely targets. Since difference is often a cause of bullying, we may question what the connection may be here. Although we cannot tell whether these views were the cause of the bullying or whether the bullying was the cause of the 'different' views, young people with different views are likely to remain in a continuing cycle of victimization and isolation. This suggests difficulties for children from religious or minority backgrounds whose traditional values may be derided. Work must be done in schools and families to build respect for the richness and diversity within our communities. However young people told us that it was often simply enough to like different music or to dress differently from other people to become targeted.

Gender

A number of young people consider that their gender affects their views on right and wrong as if these were not absolutes, applicable to all.

Drugs and police involvement

Worried about it?

■ More than two thirds of the severely bullied young men worried about the effects of drugs.

■ Significantly fewer young men who were not bullied, were worried (57%).

Pressure to try drugs

People who were severely bullied were twice as likely to report being pressurized into taking drugs by their friends. 15% of the severely bullied boys felt pressurized into trying drugs in contrast to only 7% of the boys who were not bullied. Similarly 16% of the severely bullied girls had tried drugs 'because their friends did it' compared to only 7% of those who were not bullied.

Drugs as a release

Perhaps of greater concern was that almost three times more severely bullied girls had tried drugs as a release from depression or tension than other girls.

In trouble with the police

More than one in five bullied boys had been in trouble with the police but the difference between the bullied and the non-bullied group was not significant.

This question was not asked in the girls' questionnaire.

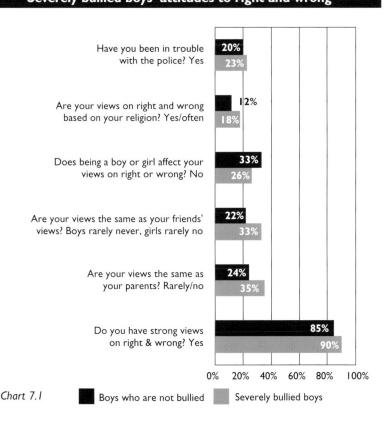

Severely bullied boys' attitudes to right and wrong

Question	Boys who are not bullied	Severely bullied boys
Have you been in trouble with the police? Yes	20%	23%
Are your views on right and wrong based on your religion? Yes/often	12%	18%
Does being a boy or girl affect your views on right or wrong? No	33%	26%
Are your views the same as your friends' views? Boys rarely never, girls rarely no	22%	33%
Are your views the same as your parents? Rarely/no	24%	35%
Do you have strong views on right & wrong? Yes	85%	90%

Chart 7.1   ■ Boys who are not bullied   ▨ Severely bullied boys

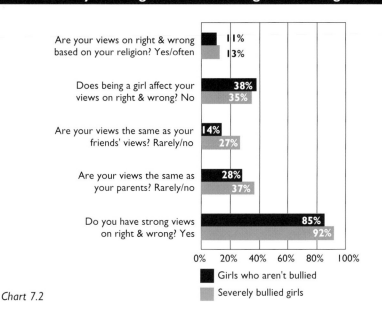

Severely bullied girls attitudes to right and wrong

Question	Girls who aren't bullied	Severely bullied girls
Are your views on right & wrong based on your religion? Yes/often	11%	13%
Does being a girl affect your views on right & wrong? No	38%	35%
Are your views the same as your friends' views? Rarely/no	14%	27%
Are your views the same as your parents? Rarely/no	28%	37%
Do you have strong views on right & wrong? Yes	85%	92%

■ Girls who aren't bullied
▨ Severely bullied girls

Chart 7.2

"I've been bullied for my religion."

Catholic Female 14

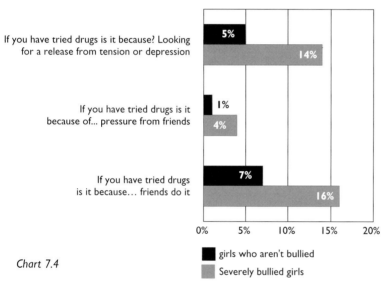

Severely bullied boys and drugs

Do you feel pressurised into trying drugs? Yes
- 7%
- 15%

Do you worry about the effects of drugs? Yes
- 57%
- 68%

0% 20% 40% 60% 80%

Chart 7.3

■ Boys who aren't bullied ■ Severely bullied boys

Severely bullied girls and drugs

If you have tried drugs is it because? Looking for a release from tension or depression
- 5%
- 14%

If you have tried drugs is it because of... pressure from friends
- 1%
- 4%

If you have tried drugs is it because... friends do it
- 7%
- 16%

0% 5% 10% 15% 20%

Chart 7.4

■ girls who aren't bullied
■ Severely bullied girls

"Bullying's getting worse now because of drugs. They want money off you for their drugs."

Male 16 Glasgow

Young Men's views on gender issues

Boys and young men who experienced severe bullying, were less comfortable with ideas about women's equality. Interviews offered a chance to talk this through. A few said they felt put down not only by the bullies but also by the increasing power of women. On the other hand, there were also suggestions that some felt very protective of their mothers whom they thought were being unfairly treated by men. Homophobic bullying which is widespread, can heighten fears or pressure a bullied boy into affecting exaggerated macho lad attitudes in order to fit in.

As seen below in chart 7.5 the survey responses show some distinct differences.

Compared to others who weren't bullied, severely bullied young men were:

■ Less likely to believe that women's equality was a good thing;

■ Less likely to agree that the level of women's equality 'has not gone far enough'.

■ Less likely to feel there was gender equality in the home.

■ More likely to say that there was 'one rule for girls and another for boys'

■ More likely to believe that there were 'more opportunities for women these days'.

Whereas 90% of those who were not bullied wanted a job and family and believed they could cope - poignantly only 73% of the severely bullied expressed this confidence. Although most young men believed that both parents should have responsibility for children, significantly fewer of the bullied agree.

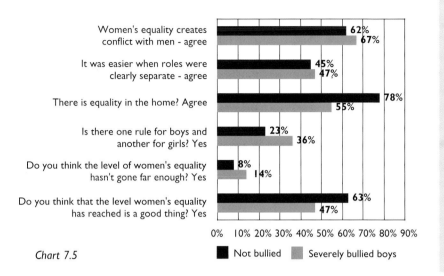

Severely bullied young men and attitudes to women's equality

Women's equality creates conflict with men - agree
- Not bullied: 62%
- Severely bullied boys: 67%

It was easier when roles were clearly separate - agree
- Not bullied: 45%
- Severely bullied boys: 47%

There is equality in the home? Agree
- Not bullied: 78%
- Severely bullied boys: 55%

Is there one rule for boys and another for girls? Yes
- Not bullied: 23%
- Severely bullied boys: 36%

Do you think the level of women's equality hasn't gone far enough? Yes
- Not bullied: 8%
- Severely bullied boys: 14%

Do you think that the level women's equality has reached is a good thing? Yes
- Not bullied: 63%
- Severely bullied boys: 47%

0% 10% 20% 30% 40% 50% 60% 70% 80% 90%

■ Not bullied ■ Severely bullied boys

Chart 7.5

> ## "You might be tempted to say 'I'll beat him up for you' but I think he should fight back himself."
>
> Girl 15 Twickenham (of her brother)

Young Women's views

The young women on the other hand, as one might expect, saw the world very differently. Nonetheless, the perspectives of the bullied and the non bullied differed:

■ Bullied girls were less confident that women's equality was a good thing.

■ They were more likely than other girls to believe that there was one rule for boys and another for girls;

■ They were more likely to agree that women's equality created conflict with men and it was easier when roles were clearly separate.

■ Significantly more of the bullied girls worried that they would only succeed by behaving like men and that they would have to be 'better than a man to succeed.'

■ They were less likely to agree that there is equality in the home and before the law;

■ They were less likely to agree that there were now 'exciting opportunities for me'.

Severely bullied young women and attitudes to women's equality

Women's equality creates conflict with men - agree
- not bullied: 79%
- Severely bullied girls: 84%

It was easier when roles were clearly separate - agree
- not bullied: 13%
- Severely bullied girls: 21%

There is equality in the home? Agree
- not bullied: 45%
- Severely bullied girls: 40%

Is there one rule for boys and another for girls? Yes
- not bullied: 33%
- Severely bullied girls: 46%

Do you think the level of women's equality has gone far enough? No, equality has not been achieved
- not bullied: 19%
- Severely bullied girls: 17%

0% 10% 20% 30% 40% 50% 60% 70% 80% 90%

■ not bullied ■ Severely bullied girls

Chart 7.6

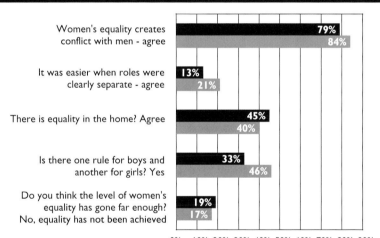

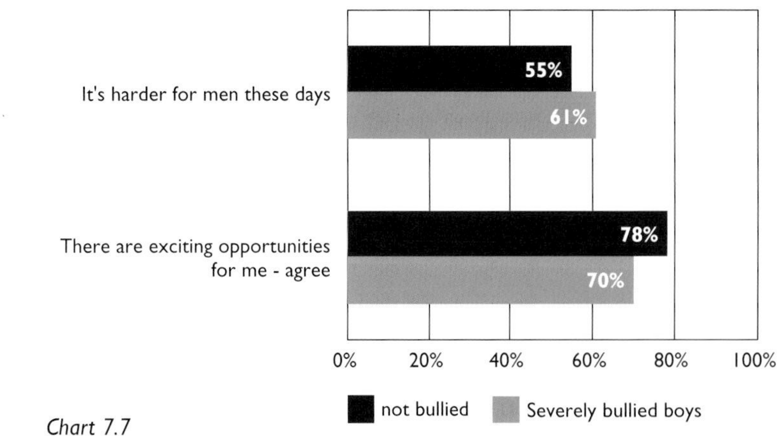

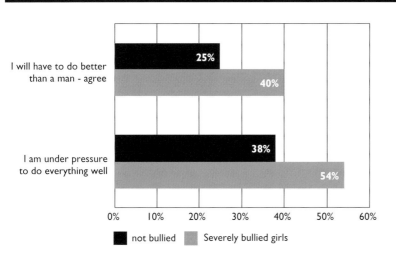

Chart 7.7

Bullied young women and attitudes to the future

Chart 7.8

contribute to a feeling of belonging. While the belief that nobody is doing anything, or can do anything about the bullying – adds to the view that 'politicians can't change anything' expressed by girls as a reason not to vote.

How does Britain seem?

Around half of all girls and boys felt Britain was a good place to live in, but both girls and boys who were bullied understandably felt significantly less positive about this. (44% and 46% respectively)

"Bullying stays with you always."

Male 17 Newcastle

"I'd say to my sisters stick up for yourselves. If anything, I was the sort who was head of my peer group."

Female 15 Twickenham

The future – pressure and anxiety

The pressures on girls to do well are reflected in chart 7.8 where over half the bullied girls feel under pressure. Boys on the other hand, in chart 7.7 demonstrate how their confidence, optimism and vision of the future is affected by having been bullied.

Citizens - concerns and actions

Generally those who were bullied tended to be more worried about public issues than those who weren't. Young women who were bullied for example, tended to be more concerned about the environment and the world situation. They thought more about

homelessness, animal rights and children's charities, and were more likely to do some voluntary work. But the differences between them and the non-bullied young people were rarely at significance level when tested.

Voting

When asked if they would vote in a general election, around two thirds of the boys said they would vote and there was little difference between the bullied and the non-bullied. On the other hand when it came to the girls 62% of the non bullied said they would vote compared to only 56% of the severely bullied girls. Making children feel protected and safe may

54

Summary:

Right and Wrong. Compared to children who weren't bullied, the severely bullied children :

- Were more likely to hold strong views on right and wrong.

- Were less likely to say that their views were the same as their friends. (Bullied girls were twice as likely to say their views were rarely or never the same.)

- More than a third said their views rarely or never coincided with their parents' views.

Drugs

- More than two thirds of boys worried about the effects of drugs.

- Both girls and boys were twice as likely to say they had been pressurised into trying drugs by their friends.

- Three times as many severely bullied girls had tried drugs as a release from tension or depression.

Police

- Bullied boys were as likely to have been in trouble with the police as non-bullied boys.

Gender equality

- Fewer than half the severely bullied boys believe that women's equality 'is a good thing'

- Severely bullied girls and boys are less likely to say 'there is equality in the home' and more likely to say there is one rule for boys and another for girls.

- More than one in five severely bullied girls believes it was easier when men and women's roles were clearly separate.

- Over half the bullied girls feel under pressure to do everything well and are much more likely to believe 'I will have to do better than a man to succeed'.

Citizens

Victims were more socially aware and concerned about public issues than those who weren't bullied. Voting intentions were little affected among boys, but bullied girls were far less likely to vote than girls who were not bullied.

Questions for classroom debate.

Are there universal rights and wrongs? What are they? Why do we need to develop a code of values? What would happen in society if we did not generally all agree on some values? Who should decide? How do we want to be treated ourselves? How do we want our teacher to treat us? How does the teacher want to be treated? Are there some subjects on which different views can be respected?

[1] Smith, P. K. & Myron-Wilson, R. 1998, Parenting & School Bullying', Clinical Child Psychology and Psychiatry. 3, 405-417

THE BULLIES

Views about right and wrong

These findings were particularly interesting. Bullies were far less likely than non-bullies to have strong views about right and wrong. When we compare these findings to the replies of victims, the different values between the victims and the bullies stand out. Whereas among severely bullied youngsters, around 90% of the boys and 92% of the girls felt they had strong views about right and wrong – among bullies, only 81% of boys and 84% of the girls said they held strong views. This is shown in charts 8.1 and 8.2.

Remarkably, most of the male bullies felt their views were the same as their parents. However, unlike the target children, there was no difference between bullies and non bullies in the percentage who thought that their views differed from those of their friends. This is worth noting because most children would say that they have very little in common with the values of bullies. These findings are also a reminder of how important it is to work with all parents in a whole school anti-bullying strategy if so many bullies feel supported at home.

Questions for Classroom debate.

If bullies believe their views on right and wrong are the same as their friends, can group discussions in class be set up to show them that this may not be true? This allows the group to coalesce around different values and dilutes the 'reward' a bully gets – popularity and power. Indirect work such as this avoids focusing on a particular event and protects the bullied child.

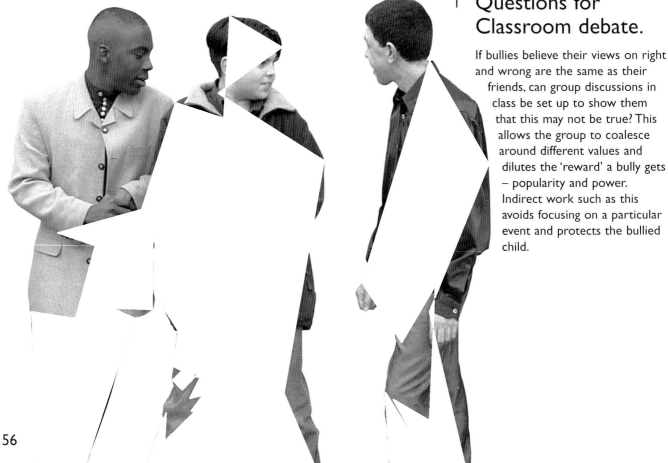

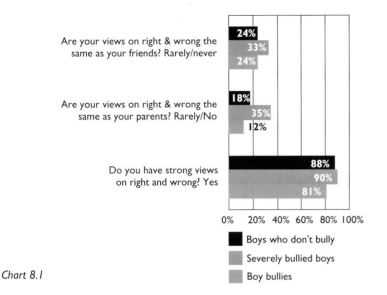

Views on right and wrong – differences between bullies, victims and boys who don't bully

Are your views on right & wrong the same as your friends? Rarely/never
24%
33%
24%

Are your views on right & wrong the same as your parents? Rarely/No
18%
35%
12%

Do you have strong views on right and wrong? Yes
88%
90%
81%

0% 20% 40% 60% 80% 100%

■ Boys who don't bully
■ Severely bullied boys
■ Boy bullies

Chart 8.1

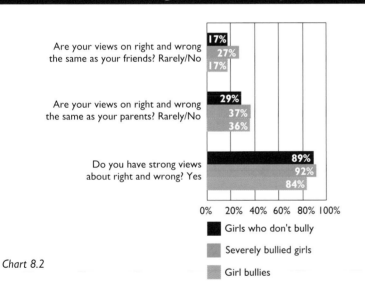

Views on right and wrong – differences between bullies, victims and girls who don't bully

Are your views on right and wrong the same as your friends? Rarely/No
17%
27%
17%

Are your views on right and wrong the same as your parents? Rarely/No
29%
37%
36%

Do you have strong views about right and wrong? Yes
89%
92%
84%

0% 20% 40% 60% 80% 100%

■ Girls who don't bully
■ Severely bullied girls
■ Girl bullies

Chart 8.2

Drugs and Police involvement

The bullies scored highly on anti-social activities in relation to non-bullies. More of the girl bullies had tried drugs to see what it was like or to get a buzz; three times as many had tried drugs looking for a release from tension or depression or to boost energy and a worrying five percent had used drugs to try and get thin. (Chart 8.4)

"I was friends with them in year seven but now they're all into drugs. One friend's on drugs and car theft and doing houses."

Male 17 Bradford

31% of boy bullies vs 16% of non bullies have tried drugs.

We have seen in Chapter seven that 15% of boys who were bullied said they had been pressurised into trying drugs. Interestingly, male bullies too report being pressurised to do this as shown in chart 8.3

There has long been a link identified between bullies and offending. 60% of former bullies have a conviction for at least one crime at the age of 24[1]. Sadly this trend can be seen starting here. This study explores replies from boys and young men between the ages of 13 and 19. Among those who admit to bullying, 31% had been in trouble with the police – twice as many as non-bullies. Over half of these bullying young men said they had been stopped by the police 'for nothing', when walking in the street. Despite this situation - remarkably - over half say they respect and trust the police. But this is significantly fewer than non-bullies.

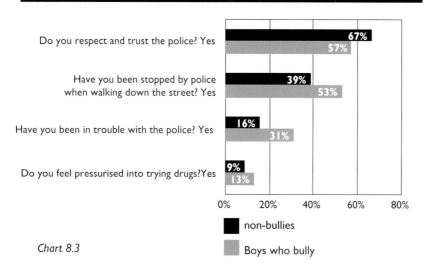

Do you respect and trust the police? Yes — 67% (non-bullies), 57% (Boys who bully)

Have you been stopped by police when walking down the street? Yes — 39% (non-bullies), 53% (Boys who bully)

Have you been in trouble with the police? Yes — 16% (non-bullies), 31% (Boys who bully)

Do you feel pressurised into trying drugs? Yes — 9% (non-bullies), 13% (Boys who bully)

■ non-bullies
■ Boys who bully

Chart 8.3

Girls who bully – if you have tried drugs was it...

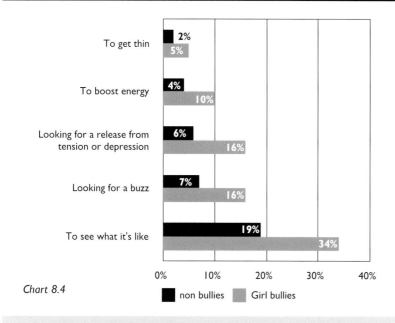

To get thin — 2% (non bullies), 5% (Girl bullies)

To boost energy — 4% (non bullies), 10% (Girl bullies)

Looking for a release from tension or depression — 6% (non bullies), 16% (Girl bullies)

Looking for a buzz — 7% (non bullies), 16% (Girl bullies)

To see what it's like — 19% (non bullies), 34% (Girl bullies)

■ non bullies   ■ Girl bullies

Chart 8.4

> ## "It's gone too far. Say in a hundred years women are in power – it will just stay that way forever."
>
> Male 14 South East

Views on gender issues

As may be expected, there were very different views about women's equality between girls and boys. There were also marked differences between the bullies and those who did not bully. Generally the boy bullies were much more negative about women's equality:

■ Boy bullies are less likely to think the level of women's equality is 'a good thing',

■ Fewer agree that the level of women's equality has 'not gone far enough';

■ They are more likely to believe that there is 'one rule for boys and another for girls.

■ They were also less likely to agree that there was equality before the law.

■ More likely to agree that it was easier when the roles for men and women were clearly separate.

■ Showing a significant difference from non-bullies, more than 80% of the boy bullies believe that men's talents are different from girls and 45% say that men are losing their rights.

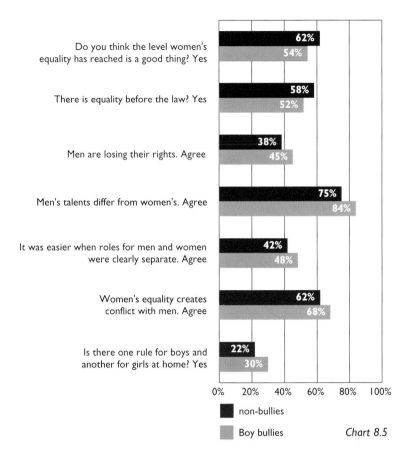

Boys who bully and attitudes to gender equality

Question	non-bullies	Boy bullies
Do you think the level women's equality has reached is a good thing? Yes	62%	54%
There is equality before the law? Yes	58%	52%
Men are losing their rights. Agree	38%	45%
Men's talents differ from women's. Agree	75%	84%
It was easier when roles for men and women were clearly separate. Agree	42%	48%
Women's equality creates conflict with men. Agree	62%	68%
Is there one rule for boys and another for girls at home? Yes	22%	30%

■ non-bullies
■ Boy bullies

Chart 8.5

As shown in chart 8.6, girls generally agree about gender equality and the differences in the beliefs held by bullies and non-bullies vary less than they do on other issues such as drugs and values. Nevertheless on issues such as equality before the law the figures tested highly significant.

Citizens. Concerns and actions

Whereas as we saw in chapter seven, the bullied children - especially the girls - were generally more caring and concerned about citizen-type issues than the non bullied. When it came to the bullies a very different picture emerged. The bullies are much less caring and concerned than the non-bullies. Perhaps in keeping with their lack of concern the girls in particular, tended to be less sure they would vote.

When it came to whether they thought Britain was a good place to live in, the boy bullies were more inclined to say no.

Bullied girls and attitudes to gender equality

Girls who bullied differed from those who did not, in several ways:

■ They were more likely to say there were different rules for boys and girls.

■ They were less likely to believe there was equality in the home and before the law.

■ They were less likely to believe that things were fairer nowadays.

■ More than 80% of both the bullies and the non-bullies felt that women's equality created conflict in with men, but despite this, over 86% of both groups felt there were exciting opportunities for them.

Girls who bully and attitudes to gender equality

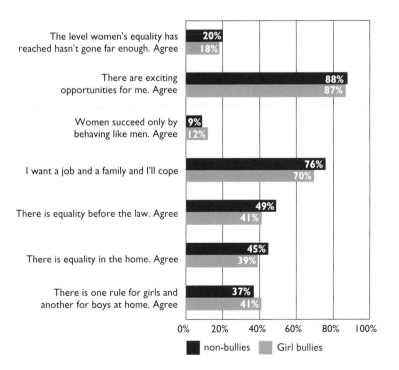

Question	non-bullies	Girl bullies
The level women's equality has reached hasn't gone far enough. Agree	20%	18%
There are exciting opportunities for me. Agree	88%	87%
Women succeed only by behaving like men. Agree	9%	12%
I want a job and a family and I'll cope	76%	70%
There is equality before the law. Agree	49%	41%
There is equality in the home. Agree	45%	39%
There is one rule for girls and another for boys at home. Agree	37%	41%

■ non-bullies
■ Girl bullies

Chart 8.6

59

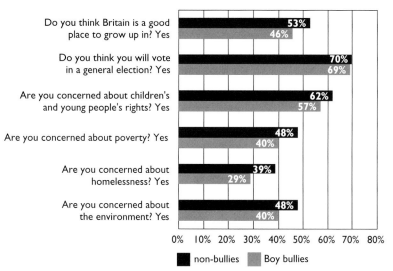

Boys who bully – attitudes to citizenship

Do you think Britain is a good place to grow up in? Yes
- non-bullies: 53%
- Boy bullies: 46%

Do you think you will vote in a general election? Yes
- non-bullies: 70%
- Boy bullies: 69%

Are you concerned about children's and young people's rights? Yes
- non-bullies: 62%
- Boy bullies: 57%

Are you concerned about poverty? Yes
- non-bullies: 48%
- Boy bullies: 40%

Are you concerned about homelessness? Yes
- non-bullies: 39%
- Boy bullies: 29%

Are you concerned about the environment? Yes
- non-bullies: 48%
- Boy bullies: 40%

■ non-bullies ■ Boy bullies

Chart 8.7

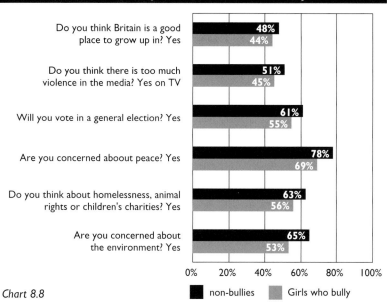

Girls who bully – attitudes to citizenship

Do you think Britain is a good place to grow up in? Yes
- non-bullies: 48%
- Girls who bully: 44%

Do you think there is too much violence in the media? Yes on TV
- non-bullies: 51%
- Girls who bully: 45%

Will you vote in a general election? Yes
- non-bullies: 61%
- Girls who bully: 55%

Are you concerned aboout peace? Yes
- non-bullies: 78%
- Girls who bully: 69%

Do you think about homelessness, animal rights or children's charities? Yes
- non-bullies: 63%
- Girls who bully: 56%

Are you concerned about the environment? Yes
- non-bullies: 65%
- Girls who bully: 53%

■ non-bullies ■ Girls who bully

Chart 8.8

Summary

Bullying is a vital social indicator. It causes ripples to go out in all directions. Although the young people who are bullied are affected with loss of self-confidence and belief in the future, bullies themselves face a number of difficulties.

■ Their views on right and wrong are less strongly held.

■ They are very likely to get into trouble with the police.

■ They are less adjusted to gender equality.

■ Their reasons for taking drugs are varied, and they show less concern for public issues or causes than other children.

■ They are less likely to play their full part in society. The social implications of bullying range far beyond the scene where it takes place and the individuals involved that day.

Questions for Classroom debate.

Why does it matter whether or not people care about the society they live in? What would happen if nobody cared about homelessness, poverty or the environment? Are there ways we can make people more aware of what belonging to a community means?

[1] Olweus, D. as above

By Victoria Bream and Ann Buchanan

'Yes, bullying has gone on for years – that doesn't make it right. We stuffed children up chimneys and down mines for years – that wasn't right either and we changed it. We can change the attitudes which allow bullying as well[1]'

Bullying is not new. The British Medical Journal notes that historically bullying in schools has either been completely ignored or has been seen as the problem of teachers and other educationalists. More recently, however, young people have make us re-think our attitudes. For many being bullied is literally a life wrecker.[2]

CHILDREN AND YOUNG PEOPLE WHO ARE BULLIED

What is bullying?

Some of the most influential research on bullying has been undertaken by Olweus in Norway. His definition is:

When a young person is exposed repeatedly and over time to intentional, negative, aggressive behaviour from an individual or group. This can be physical, verbal, spreading rumours or by excluding someone. Bullying involves an imbalance of power.

It is also bullying when a young person is teased repeatedly. But it is not bullying when two young people of the same strength have the odd fight or quarrel'[3] There are aggressive interchanges when two young people don't know one another, or they fight in a queue for example, but these are different to bullying.

How common is the experience of being bullied?

Bullying is widespread. In the United Kingdom, 27% of junior and middle school pupils and 10% of secondary school pupils said that they had been bullied sometimes or more often that term. A further 10% and 4% respectively said that they were bullied more than once a week.[4] The national anti-bullying campaign helpline receives 16,000 calls every year from distressed pupils[5].

Tell-tale signs that a child is being bullied

Michelle Elliot[6] lists the following signs that may indicate that a child or young person is being bullied:

Signs that a child or young person is being bullied

Children or young people may:

- Be frightened if walking to or from school
- Be unwilling to go to school and make continual excuses to avoid going
- Beg to be driven to school
- Change their route to school every day
- Begin doing poorly in their schoolwork
- Regularly have clothes or books or schoolwork torn or destroyed
- Come home starving (because dinner money was taken)
- Become withdrawn
- Start stammering
- Start acting out or hitting other children (as a reaction to being bullied by those children or others)
- Stop eating or become obsessively clean (as a reaction to be called 'fatty' or 'dirty')
- Develop stomach and headaches due to stress
- Attempt suicide
- Cry themselves to sleep
- Begin wetting the bed
- Have nightmares and call out things like, 'leave me alone'
- Have unexplained bruises, scratches, cuts
- Have their possessions go 'missing'
- Ask for money or begin stealing money (to pay the bully)
- Continually 'lose' their pocket money
- Refuse to say what's wrong
- Give improbable excuses to explain any of the above[7]

What are the mental health consequences for young people?

Victims of bullying experience various forms of distress and disruption to their lives. The effects on mental health of being bullied are serious – young people who are bullied more are more likely to be depressed. Popular concepts of bullied children are that they are anxious, scared and have low self-esteem. However, meta-analysis shows that the largest effect on children is depression, and the smallest is anxiety.[8]

Young people who have been victimised by their peers are twice as likely as non-victims to report suicidal thoughts and other symptoms of depression[9]. When asked to rate their happiness, bullied children are generally less happy than children who have not been victimised by their peers[10].

Children who are depressed may become part of a negative

reinforcing cycle. Young people who are more introverted, less assertive and over-involved with their families are particularly vulnerable to bullies[11]. Or, because a young person is depressed, he/she may also attract more negative attention from their peers. Victims of bullying are likely to be lonely. Bullied children have lower self-esteem, and a more negative view of their social competence[12]. All these negative consequences occur amongst both boys and girls, in all age groups and as a result of all kinds of bullying.

What effect does bullying have on school work?

Bullying not only causes severe distress, it also affects how children do in school. The Department for Education and Employment says that:

'The emotional distress caused by bullying in whatever form – be it racial, or a result of a child's appearance, behaviour or special

educational needs, or related to sexual orientation – can prejudice school achievement, lead to lateness or truancy and, in extreme cases, end with suicide.

A third of girls and a quarter of boys are at some time afraid of going to school because of bullying.

Bullying is usually part of a pattern of behaviour rather than an isolated incident. Pupils should be encouraged to report any bullying to staff or to older pupils they can trust.

Low report rates should not of themselves be taken as proof that bullying is not occurring'[13]

What are the long term effects?

As well as the short and medium term psychological and physical harm that results from bullying[14], bullying can have longer term effects. It has been found that boys who had been victimised has much higher levels of depression and a more negative view of themselves at 23 years of age[15]. Bullying may also be associated with later alcohol problems and family violence[16]; additionally there is evidence of intergenerational continuity of victimisation[17].

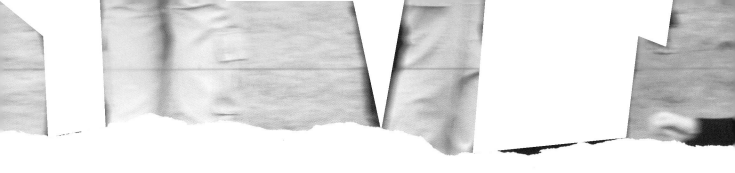

THE BULLIES

Why do children bully each other?

In the process of growing up, both at home and at primary school, the child has to learn non-aggressive ways of interacting with his/her peers. Initially, young children might bully others as they don't know that it is wrong. By secondary school, if not long before, most young people will understand that bullying is not an acceptable behaviour in school, nor elsewhere.

But children and young people are surrounded by mixed messages. When parents, media role models, other adults, as well as peers are seen to use bullying-type behaviour the message is that bullying behaviour is OK. This message is reinforced when young people see that bullies are seldom punished. In effect they see it is acceptable. They also learn that it is an effective strategy: bullies get what they want and they get away with it.[18]

Bullies are also more popular than victims. This provides fertile breeding ground for creating new bullies. To be popular, children can be persuaded by their friends to bully a more vulnerable person.

Young people may be reluctant to help others who are being bullied. There is a deep fear of 'grassing'. When young people get involved, they risk becoming victims themselves; they risk their own safety. Observational studies show that pupils not involved in a bullying situation, may not intervene. Worse still, they may later join in themselves[19]. It is safer to be part of the 'gang'.

Studies of the families of bullies also suggest there are parenting factors which may also reinforce bullying behaviour. The families of bullies have been found to be more distant, less warm and exercising inconsistent discipline[20].

Some children might bully others over a period of time when they are experiencing difficulties at home or at school. In effect, although this does not condone the behaviour, they are acting out their own troubled feelings[21].

Some bullies pay the price

Bullying other children is one of the major causes of exclusion from school. Government statistics show that 30.1% of exclusions are due to bullying, fighting and assaults on peers, with a further 14.9% due to verbal abuse to peers[22].

Perhaps surprisingly, depression has been found to occur both amongst those who are bullied and those who are doing the bullying. It is most common among those who have been involved in both. When symptoms of depression were controlled for, suicidal ideation occurred most often among adolescents who were bullies[23]. A cross-sectional study carried out with adolescent children in Australia found associations between bullying behaviour and psychosomatic symptoms and smoking, both for those young people who bullied and those who were victims of bullying. Bullies tended to report being unhappy with school. Those individuals who bullied and bully themselves had the most psychological and psychosomatic symptoms, often disliking school and feeling alone. [24]

Different types of bullying

Hawker & Boulton[25] describe three subtypes of victimisation, derived from social rank theory:

1. physical victimisation e.g. hitting, kicking

2. relational victimisation e.g. being excluded from relationships and activities

3. verbal victimisation e.g. direct: malicious teasing, name-calling; indirect: rumour spreading

As well as these familiar types of threatening and violent behaviour, young people are also involved in specific racist and homophobic bullying:

'Racist violence, harassment and abuse are closely related to, and sometimes difficult to distinguish from, bullying.

Racist bullying in schools can range from ill-considered remarks, which are not intended to be hurtful, to deliberate physical attacks causing serious injury.

Racist bullying can be identified by the motivation of the bully, the language used, and/or by the fact that victims are singled out because of the colour of their skin, the way they talk, their ethnic grouping or by their religious or cultural practices'[26]

Homophobic bullying is widespread and the victims can be of any sexual orientation.

'Homophobic bullying can involve physical or mental violence by a group or an individual. It is usually aimed at someone who has poor defences and who, as a result, may be significantly upset. What distinguishes it from other forms of bullying is the language that is used and the motivation of those who are doing the bullying.'[27]

The anti-bullying network describe how homophobic bullying can be a major problem[28]:

■ children who experience it have their education disrupted. They may be unable to concentrate on lessons because of feelings of fear and anger. Their self-confidence may be damaged and, as a result, they may never fulfil their academic potential

■ it can be a particular problem for teenagers who are confused or unsure about their own developing sexuality. Some victims are driven to the edge of despair or beyond with lasting consequences for their emotional health and development

■ schools that ignore it, or deny its existence, are not helping young people to develop a concern for the welfare of minorities and a tolerance of difference

Differences between boys and girls

Girls spend more time with friends than boys do, so are more likely to be disturbed by relational aggression[29]. Girls might perceive certain behaviours as bullying, whereas boys would not report the same behaviour in the same way.

In a study of peer support programmes, Naylor & Cowie[30] found that in all-boy schools there was a surplus of volunteer pupils and volunteer male staff. However, in mixed schools there was a lack of male volunteers amongst teachers and pupils, while females were eager to volunteer. This shows the profound effects of context on whether boys felt able to show the more sensitive side of their nature:

"...it seems that boys can 'care'. What does seem to be the case, however, is that many boys, particularly early adolescents, do not choose to use their caring abilities, or to seek out care from a peer supporter, unless they perceive that the circumstances in which they are to do so will not threaten their perception of what it is to be masculine."

The legal requirements

Since September 1999 head-teachers have had a specific obligation to take measures to prevent all forms of bullying amongst pupils, as part of their school's discipline and behaviour policy:

(4) The head teacher shall determine measures (which may include the making of rules and provision for enforcing them) to be taken with a view to –

(b) Encouraging good behaviour and respect for others on the part of pupils and, in particular, preventing all forms of bullying among pupils

(7) The measures determined by the head teacher under subsection (4) shall be publicised by him in the form of a written document as follows-

(a) He shall make the measures generally known within the school and to parents of the registered pupils at the school; and

(b) He shall in particular, at least once in every school year, take steps to bring them to the attention of all such pupils and parents and to all persons employed, or otherwise engaged to provide services, at the school[31]

Peer support systems

Research suggests that it is important to include the entire peer group in anti-bullying strategy. Peers spend a large proportion of their time in the playground passively watching bullying, tacitly reinforcing the bullying behaviour as acceptable or even desirable. Thus there is a need to heighten awareness of the negative aspects of bullying, and foster a peer culture that opposes bullying-type behaviour. However, it is important that the opposition to bullying is not seen to be aggressive itself[32].

Key features of anti-bullying programmes in schools

Anti-bullying programmes in schools generally have these features in common:

1: they have a school policy specifically targeting bullying and also procedures for dealing with incidents of bullying when they arise.

2: these procedures are typically teacher-directed.

3: they employ a combination of counselling students who are involved

4: and sanctions to punish bullies and deter further bullying behaviour.

Some schools, however, enable students themselves to contribute towards a solution to the bullying problem. There are a variety of reasons for doing this.

Children who are victimised often prefer to go to other students for help rather than to teachers. This is particularly true of children in secondary schools, where fewer than one in four of the children who indicated in surveys that they have been bullied report having ever informed a teacher compared with more than half who have spoken about it to another student (Rigby 1997)'[33]

A large scale survey of teachers' and pupils perceptions gives a useful insight into why and how such systems can work[34]. Pupil supporters are trained in listening and problem-solving skills that they use in a confidential setting.

'Peer supporter initiatives need to be sustainable. A 'cascade' of training for peer supporters is ideal whereby older, established peer supporters are involved in the training and initial mentoring of a new, younger group of peer supporters. Consistent adult supervision and support of this process is important to provide continuity, safety and structure when necessary without 'taking over' the process.'[35]

Features of peer support systems

1: There is a direct response from the peer to a request for help from a student.

2: The peer helpers are given skills and strategies for enabling the young people involved in the situation to find a resolution to the problem.

3: Adults retain a supportive and supervisory role … though the direct action is taken by the peer helpers.

4: There are non-punitive interventions which offer clear channels of communication amongst those involved in the situation.

5: All of the interventions assume that pupils themselves have the potential to adopt a helpful role in relation to peers in distress.

6: All take place outside the classroom, and so depend on the school having the resources and commitment to facilitate the peer support system'[36]

Adequate supervision is key. The benefits of peer support programmes have been found to be compromised if the programme is not adequately supervised. Peer supporters can be harassed by other pupils, and teachers running the programmes can experience hostility from other staff members[37].

There is a risk too that peer supporters can be over-burdened by a child who has severe problems that are beyond the supporter's competence.

Mentoring

Another approach suggested by the Department for Education and Employment as a measure to counter bullying is mentoring:

'Older pupils can sometimes support or offer a role model for pupils who need help and guidance, particularly after poor behaviour or in cases where they risk failure at school because of bullying by others'[38]

Home-school agreements

Some schools have introduced home-school agreements, clarifying responsibilities and expectations from both parties with respect to combating bullying[39].

The whole-school approach to bullying

The approach that appears to be the most effective, is one that that involves the whole school and parents and the wider community[40]. The initiative for this may come from the teachers, the parents or the children themselves. A whole school approach towards bullying should make it difficult for bullying once detected or reported to continue as the combined forces of school, parents and the community are there to ensure that it is simply not tolerated.

Key stages in developing the whole school approach

1: The survey: students fill in an anonymous questionnaire on the extent of bullying and the problems it causes.

2: Staff meeting: staff meet and discuss the results of the survey and plan how to tell students.

3: Class rules. Each class is asked to write down five rules that they would like everybody in the school to live by.

4: School rules. A group of students put together a list of rules from those given by the classes.

5: Staff approval: teachers meet with students and make any adjustments necessary to the proposed rules

6: Student approval: Suggested rules are referred back to pupils for a secret vote.

7: School contract. A common contract signed by each student.

8: School governors agree rules

9: Parents. Perhaps meeting with parents to say the rules have been agreed and to ask them to sign a contract supporting the rules.

10: Local authority informed. Their support may be necessary if the school needs backing for suspending a student for bullying (Adapted from Michelle Elliot 1991)

The whole school approach does not end with the signing of the contracts. The message will have to be continually reinforced in school assemblies, on notice boards, when staff are supervising students in free-time, when teaching the curriculum and at parent meetings. As part of the school policy there will be consequences or sanctions meted out to those who break the rules.

'By setting up a whole-school approach to eliminating bullying, you are sending signals to the children that you do care about their welfare. This approach assumes good pupil-staff relations and creates and atmosphere which continues to foster those relationships. Involving parents and the community will help to change attitudes which encourage bullying'[41].

Signs that an anti-bullying policy is working

One of the apparent paradoxes is that as the profile of bullying is raised more incidents of bullying will be reported by pupils. Initially, therefore, bullying rates may appear to increase rather than decrease. The following indicators will suggest that an anti-bullying policy is working:

- an increased confidence of students to report bullying

- an increased willingness of teaching and ancillary staff to intervene in bullying incidents

- the development of a shared perception by adults and students of those behaviours which cannot be tolerated, and those which cannot[42]

How young people's views can help us know what to do

Views have changed since the child was felt to be the 'most unreliable of all witnesses'[43]. Today, quite apart from children's rights under The Convention[44], it could be said to be dangerous, as evidenced by the recent Lost in Care report of child abuse in residential homes in Wales[45], not to listen to what young people have to say. When it comes to the bullied and those who bully, we need to hear what is said, not only because it may be dangerous not to, but also because they are the experts in their situation.

This study was a result of three confidential questionnaires on the views and experiences of young people age 13 to 19 from all over Britain, undertaken with girls in 1996 and with boys in 1998. Findings from a third survey taken in March 2000 include responses from girls and boys.

CONCLUSION

There is now a great deal of reliable information available about bullying and bullies in school: the extent of the problem; the distress it causes and the short and long term consequences. There is now also considerable evidence of what can be done to counteract and prevent the problems. Bullying should be a problem of yesterday. Sadly as the findings from this survey of young people shows it is not. Bullying and being bullied is still rife in our schools.

[1] Elliott, M. (1997) Ed. 'Bullying: A practical guide to coping for schools'. Second edition, Prentice Hall.

[2] Chesson, R. (1999) Bullying: the need for an interagency response British Medical Journal 319 330-331.

[3] Smith, P.K. & Sharp, S. (Eds) (1994) School Bullying: Insights and Perspectives. London, Routledge. Definition adapted from Olweus, D. (1991) Bully / victim problems amongst school children: basic facts and effects of a school-based intervention programme. In D. Pepler & K. Rubin (Eds) The Development and Treatment of Childhood Aggression. Hillsdale, NJ: Erlbaum.

[4] Chesson, R as above.

[5] Chesson R as above.

[6] Elliott, M. (1997) Ed. 'Bullying: A practical guide to coping for schools'. Second edition, Prentice Hall.

[7] Elliott as above.

[8] Hawker, D.S.J. & Boulton, M.J. (2000) 'Twenty Years' Research on Peer Victimization and Psychosocial Maladjustment: A Meta-analytic Review of Cross-sectional Studies' Journal of Child Psychology and Psychiatry and Allied Disciplines, 4, 441-455.

[9] Rigby, K. (1996) 'Bullying in schools: And what to do about it' London: Jessica Kingsley.

[10] Rigby, K. & Slee, P.T. (1992) 'Dimensions of interpersonal relation among Australian children and implications for psychological well-being.' The Journal of Social Psychology, 133 33-42.; Williams, K., Chambers, M., Logan, S., & Robinson, D. (1996) 'Association of common health symptoms with bullying in primary school children' British Medical Journal 313, 17-19.

[11] Bowers, L., Smith, P.K., Binney, V. (1994) Perceived family relationships of bullies, victims and bully/victims in middle childhood Journal of Social Personal Relationships 11: 215-232.

[12] Hawker and Boulton see above.

[13] DfEE (1999) Chapter 4 paragraph 29 Handling signs of Disaffection.

[14] Chesson, R as above.

[15] Olweus, D. (1994) Bullying at school: basic facts and effects of a school based intervention program Journal of child Psychology and Psychiatry and Allied Disciplines 35: 1171-1190.

[16] Kaltiala-Heino R, Rimpela M., Marttunen M., Rimpela, A, Rantanen, P (NB ACCENTS) Bullying, depression, and suicidal ideation in Finnish adolescents: school survey British Medical Journal 1999 319: 348-351.

[17] Bernstein, J.M. & Watson, M.J. (1997) Journal of Interpersonal Violence 12 438-498.

[18] O'Connell, P., Pepler, D. & Craig, W (1999) Peer Involvement in bullying; insights and challenges for intervention Journal of Adolescence 22 437-452.

[19] O'Connell et al (1997) Prevalence of bullying and victimization among Canadian elementary and middle school children Poster session presented at the meeting of the Society for Research in Child Development, Washington D.C.

[20] Bowers, as above.

[21] DfEE (2000) Out of school – Health and Welfare - Bullying.

[22] Truancy and School Exclusion Report by the Social Exclusion Unit (1998) Cabinet Office.

[23] Kaltiala-Heino.

[24] Forero, R., McLellan, L., Rissel, C. & Bauman, A. (1999) Bullying Behaviour and psychosocial health among school students in New South Wales, Australia: cross sectional survey British Medical Journal 319 344-348.

[25] Hawker, D. S.J. & Boulton, M.J. (2000?) 'Peer Harassment in school' ed. Juvonen, J & Graham, S. New York: Guilford.

[26] Information on racist bullying: Anti-bullying network.

[27] Information for schools about homophobic bullying Anti-bullying network.

[28] as 23.

[29] Cunningham et al (1998) The effects of primary division, student mediated conflict resolution programs on playground aggression Journal of Child Psychology and Psychiatry 39 653-662.

[30] Naylor, P & Cowie, H. (1999). 'The effectiveness of peer support systems in challenging school bullying: the perspectives and experiences of teachers and pupils'. Journal of Adolescence 22, 467-479.

[31] School Standards and Framework Act 1998.

[32] O'Connell (1999) as above.

[33] Peterson, L & Rigby, K (1997) 'Countering bullying at an Australian secondary school with students as helpers' journal of Adolescence 22 481-492.

[34] Naylor, P & Cowie, H (1999) 'The effectiveness of peer support systems in challenging school bullying: the perspectives and experiences of teachers and pupils' Journal of adolescence 22 467-479.

[35] Turner, G. (1999) 'Peer support and young people's health' Journal of Adolescence 22 567-572.

[36] Sharp, S. & Cowie, H. (1998) Counselling and supporting children in distress London: Sage.

[37] Cowie, H. (1998) Perspectives of teachers and pupils on the experience of peer support against bullying Educational Research and Evaluation, 4 108-125.

[38] DfEE (1999) Handling signs of Disaffection.

[39] DfEE (1999) Handling signs of Disaffection.

[40] Besag, V. Bullies and Victims in Schools. Open University Press; Roland E. and Munthe, E. (eds.) Bullying, an international perspective. David Fulton Publishers.

[41] Elliott, M. (1997) Ed. 'Bullying: A practical guide to coping for schools'. Second edition, Prentice Hall. Page 166-171.

[42] Home Office Police Policy Directorate Police Research Group 'Preventing school bullying: things you can do (Schools Edition).

[43] Goodman, G. A. (1984). Children's testimony in Historial Perspective. Journal of Social Issues, 40, 2, 9-31.

[44] United Nations 1989 UN Convention on the Rights of the Child New York United Nations.

[45] Department of Health (2000) Lost in Care Report. www.doh.gov.uk/lostincare/20157.htm

"Bullies make you do something you don't want to do. Bullies make people scared. They should teach how to stand up to them and the bully would back off."

Male prisoner 21

Half our future

The central message from this research is that more than half of all children had been bullied and more than one in ten had been severely victimized. Torment and victimisation in our schools is an everyday living hell for many young people. These young people constitute half our future.

This is not the whole story. In addition to severe bullying, almost all children have been subjected to name-calling and other taunts, and witnessing and experiencing racism is a daily experience for many.

The costs are not only to the young people themselves but also to society as a whole. Young people who are bullied are more likely to be depressed and suicidal (one in 5 of the severely bullied had attempted suicide), more likely to be alienated from school and perhaps as a result more likely to underachieve. Their own experience of victimization both at school and in the home is associated with a greater willingness to think it is acceptable to use violence to discipline a child, leading to continuing patterns of victimization in the next generation.

> **"This PE teacher would call out 'come on you fatso, get up and run' - to this boy who had asthma and couldn't do sport. It happened every time."**
>
> Boy 15 Liverpool

The second message is that the bullied have much in common with those who are bullies: depression/suicidal thoughts and attempts; parents with punitive parenting styles; considerable experience of violence, different views about right and wrong. The bullies are more likely to be involved in antisocial activities and illegal drugs and alcohol. They are generally less concerned and caring citizens. Many of the bullies have themselves been victimized.

The other half of all our future, those who were neither bully nor bullied - are altogether happier, more productive and positive future citizens. How can we make this the experience of all children?

The following table summarises some of the factors associated with the bullied and the bullies.

Key	
+	Significant positive associations
-	Significant negative associations
ND	No data
NS	Not significant

So what does all this mean?

The young people who have spoken out in this study give us many clues as to how we can rid our schools of the living hell many children experience. Preventing bullying, however, probably starts long before school entry.

In the child's earliest days parents can lay the foundations that will protect a child from being bullied and in turn protect that child from being a bully. Children who experience positive parenting strategies and non-violent ways to resolve conflict are less likely be at risk of being bullied or being bullies. Schools can continue the good work with comprehensive anti-bullying policies, but it is not enough to have the policies they need - they must have policies that work. There is room for considerable improvement in the number of schools that have effective policies. But when all these fail, young people need someone to somebody to talk to. For the bullied this may just make the difference between surviving the torment or never escaping it.

Table: Emotional support –where would you go? Boys

	Severely bullied	Less severely	Not bullied
If extremely upset would you phone a helpline? – 'yes'	31.0 (53)	27.8 (159)	19.8 (100)
If you wouldn't phone a helpline why?			
– people will think I'm useless	10.0 (12)	4.6 (19)	2.8 (11)
– they can't do anything about my life	26.7 (32)	29.7 (123)	21.5 (84)
– would you prefer to use an email helpline instead of a telephone helpline? – 'yes'	30.2 (51)	19.9 (114)	19.8 (98)

THE BULLIES

The tragedy for the bullies is that they do not yet realize that they too need help.

	Have bullied	Never bullied
If extremely upset would you phone a helpline? – 'yes'	24.8 (111)	25.0 (200)
If you wouldn't phone a helpline why?		
– people will think I'm useless	4.5 (15)	4.6 (27)
– I don't really understand how they work	7.1 (24)	10.7 (63)
– they can't do anything about my life	26.7 (32)	29.7 (123)
– boys don't do this	14.3 (48)	9.7 (57)
– would you prefer to use an email helpline instead of a telephone helpline? – 'yes'	19.9 (89)	22.2 (175)

> **"If you're wearing a nice cap it gets nicked off ya every time. Society isn't protecting children, there should be more police patrols. If you've been bullied it stays with you. If I were a father, I'd say to a kid - come and talk to me."**
>
> 17 Newcastle

> **"To be honest, I think bullying is going to happen no matter what."**
>
> Boy 17 Twickenham

Methodology

The survey respondents

Data for this study were collected as part of confidential questionnaires researching the views and experiences of boys and girls aged between 13 and 19. The questionnaires were devised by Adrienne Katz in consultation with a range of children's agencies and Ann Buchanan at Oxford University, with help from youth workers, therapists, researchers and young people.

The girls' questionnaire was circulated with help from the Sunday Express colour magazine on September 1st 1996. In addition 20,000 were circulated to voluntary organisations, schools and youth clubs. By closing date, four weeks later 5000 replies had been received. NSM Research arranged 3000 of the replies into a demographically representative scheme, by area, considering the age groups needed and showing family structure. After the publication of the first set of results, the dataset was moved to Oxford University.

The boys' questionnaire was circulated with help from The Express on March 16, 1998. To control for possible newspaper response bias, additional questionnaires were distributed in schools and youth clubs and a control group examined. 1344 boys replied to the survey. Initial data entry was undertaken by National Opinion Polls, and then the data set was transferred to Oxford University for further analysis.

The boys' questionnaire was constructed to be comparable with that of the girls. Some wording was marginally different, especially where the responses from the first study (the girls) had been a little confusing. Where there are minor differences in the wording these are indicated.

Young people answered the questionnaire anonymously and there was a freepost address provided. It is considered that, for teenagers answering this type of questionnaire, anonymity is a requirement. Those who agreed to personal interviews did so with the agreement that their words could be used without their name, either anonymously or with a pseudonym.

To check recent trends in bullying, further data from a third survey were subsequently considered. This was undertaken in March 2000 with support from Sky Television and included both girls and boys. Questionnaires were delivered to schools, youth services and a range of other groups and institutions nationwide. 2722 replies were received.

The responses came from the following regions:

Surveys 1. 1996 2. 1998 3. 2000	Scotland	N. Ireland	Wales	North West	North East	South West	South East	Midlands	
1. Girls	6%	1%	5%	15%	11%	9%	36%	17%	
2. Boys	5%	1%	3%	27%	8%	8%	24%	16%	
3. Boys & Girls	4%	1%	2%	18%	13%	2%	SE not London: 18% London: 25%	6%	East incl E. Anglia 7%

The Bullied - How the groups were derived

In data from the first two surveys, three levels of victimized young people were derived. Those who had experienced extreme levels of bullying: those who had experienced 'a middle' level and those who had no bullying or only mild.

Boys	Extreme	Middle	Mild / Never
Have you been physically attacked? OR	A lot	A little	Never
Have you been threatened with violence? OR	A lot	A little	Never
Have you been picked on by a group?	A lot	A bit	Never

Girls	Extreme	Middle	Mild / Never
Have you been physically attacked? OR	A lot	A bit	Never
Have you been pushed or punched? OR	A lot	A bit	Never
Have you been threatened with violence? OR	A lot	A bit	Never
Have you been victimised by a group?	A lot	A bit	Never

The variable was designed to include all young people who had answered the questionnaire.

The categories were mutually exclusive in that to be included in the 'middle' category, the respondent had to NOT be in the extreme category AND answer the questions as shown in the table; similarly, to be in the 'mild' category, the respondent had to NOT be in the middle or extreme category AND answer the questions as shown in the table.

The numbers in each group

The following table shows the numbers and percentages in each group.

Level of bullying - victim				
Level of bullying	Boys	%	Girls	%
Extreme	176	13.1	359	12.0
Middle	599	44.6	1273	42.4
Mild	536	39.9	1360	45.3
Not answered	33	2.5	8	0.3
Total	1344	100%	3000	100%

The bullies

The group for the Bullies was derived from replies to the question, 'Have you bullied someone else?' A little, A lot From these questions the following numbers were obtained.

Bullies				
Level of bullying	Boys	%	Girls	%
Have bullied	469	34.9	783	26.1
Never bullied	842	62.6	2203	73.4
Not answered	33	2.5	14	0.5
Total		1344	100%	3000	100%

> ## "I used to hang around with some people who used to bully. But I never used to do it. There is more bullying now generally."
>
> Girl 16 Twickenham

The group of young people who answered 'a lot' was very small, so the answers 'a lot' and 'a little' were grouped together. Very different levels of bullying behaviour may be represented in this 'catch-all' category. The group of young people who answered 'a lot' would be a very interesting subgroup to study.

Other derived variables Family togetherness

	High Family Togetherness	Low Family Togetherness
How often do you eat a meal together? AND	Daily	Sometimes / Never
How often do you visit friends and relatives together? AND	Daily	Sometimes / Never
How often do you go out for a walk or play sport together	Daily	Sometimes / Never

	High family togetherness	Low family togetherness
Boys	27% (368)	14% (187)
Girls	22% (656)	6% (168)

Father involvement

Does your dad/father figure:	High Father Involvement	Low Father Involvement
Spend time with you? AND	Yes	Sometimes / No
Show an interest in your schoolwork? AND	Yes	Sometimes / No
Talk through your worries with you?	Yes	Sometimes / No

	High Father Involvement	Low Father Involvement
Boys	22% (290)	7% (92)
Girls	No data available	No data available

Limitations of the study

Within the broad groups there will of course be individuals who do not conform to the suggested patterns. The findings only give us some indication of the broad characteristics of each group.

A dilemma in this study, is that respondents were self-selected – they chose to answer the questionnaire, and despite the national distribution, the sample may not be truly representative. Various comparisons with different groups increase the confidence in the quality of the data.

In the boys study it was possible to compare responses from a group of young men surveyed in schools. The only significant differences between the two groups related to age… as might be expected the school group was younger.

Findings from the 1998 boys' survey also compared well with the Sky data collected two years later in the third survey.

Following the self-selected and self-reported nature of the study, some variables may be under-reported; depression can be related to feelings of social isolation and hopelessness – potential

respondents may not have gained access to a questionnaire due to spending a lot of time alone, or may have felt that their opinion wouldn't make any difference. Anti-school attitudes can be related to poor academic ability or performance, the literacy required to read and complete the questionnaire would have excluded some adolescent boys from responding. Adolescent boys in young offenders' institutions and residential homes may not have had access to the 1998 questionnaire, so in this way the proportion of young men involved with the police will be under-reported. More young people in these circumstances were reached in the third survey, which also offered respondents the use of a cassette recording of the questionnaire.

[1] Buchanan, A. et al. *Answering Back. The Views of Young People being Looked after.* University of Southampton, CEDR.

[2] Buchanan, A. et al. (2000) In and out of behaviour problems in Buchanan A. and Hudson, B. L. Promoting the Emotion Well-being of Children, Oxford: Oxford University Press. Buchanan, A. and Ten Brinke, J.A. (1998) *'Recovery from Emotional and Behavioural Problems'*, NHS, Anglia and Oxford.

Conclusions

Accessing the views of young people is always difficult. Evidence suggests that marginally different responses will be elicited by different approaches – for example whether young people are interviewed direct (interview bias) or in groups (group bias).[1] Surveys undertaken in school reflect only those who are at school. The newspaper route although imperfect, offered complete confidentiality. In addition, as the responses demonstrated, it was effective in attracting replies from young people not in school. These may be the very young people who were not in school because they were being victimized.

It is encouraging that some of the findings from the data reflect findings from work by Buchanan and Ten

Brinke (1998) using longitudinal data from the 17 000 representative people who took part in the National Child Development Study.[2] Some of the findings from the first two surveys for this study are also reflected in the third survey, of 2,722 boys and girls undertaken in 2000 for Young Voice. Replies came from schools, youth services, hostels care situations and young men on remand. They came from all over Britain. Each study can only add another piece of jigsaw to the overall picture. When separate studies undertaken with different samples using different methods reflect similar findings, confidence grows that the messages from the young people who took part here reflect a reality for young people in Britain today. If we are to limit the consequences of bullying, we do well to listen to the messages they are giving.

Resources

Books

Cowie, H. & Sharp, S. (1996) **Peer Counselling in Schools: a Time to Listen** London: David Fulton

Cowie, H. & Wallace, P. (2000) **Peer Support in Action: from Bystanding to Standing By** London: Sage.

Peer support in action is a useful and insightful aid for teachers, educational psychologists and all professionals involved in the pastoral care and guidance of children and young people. The authors combine insights drawn from practice with up to date research findings to give a sound basis for peer-based interventions.
For more information see related email site

DfEE new edition (2001) **Don't suffer in silence** London: HMSO

Sharp, S. & Cowie, H. (1998) **Counselling and Supporting Children in Distress** London: Sage.

Sharp, S. & Cowie, H. (1994) **Tackling Bullying through the curriculum** In P.K.

Smith and Sharp, S. (eds) **School Bullying: Insights & Perspectives** London: Routledge.

Sharp, S. & Cowie, H. (1994) **Tackling bullying in your school** London: Routledge

Tattum, D. & Tattum, E. **Bullying The Early Years, Advice for Parents, Teachers and Carers** Cardiff: University of Wales Institute

Helplines and Organisations that Help

Anti-Bullying Campaign
185 Tower Bridge Road
London SE1 2UF
020 7378-1446
ACE exclusion helpline
020 7704-9822

Anti-bullying infoline.

The line of the anti-bullying network at the University of Edinburgh.
0131 651-6100
9.30a.m. –12.30p.m. and 2 p.m. – 4.30p.m. during school terms.
For learning more about how bullying can be tackled or where to go for advice. This is not a counselling or mediation service.
Email abn@mhie.ac.uk
For more information see related email site

Childline 0800 1111

Childline Bullying Line 0800 44 1111

Children's Legal Centre
Advice on Children's Legal Rights
020 7359-6251

Child Protection
0800 800-500

Durham County Council Anti-Bullying Policy and Guidelines. A council wide innovative scheme involving peer participation and all those acting on behalf of the council. Bullying is identified as an important area of activity in the LEA's Behaviour plan.

KIDSCAPE forerunners in educating schools, parents and children on issues around bullying. Tel: 0207 730-3300 Mon & Wed 9.30 –4.30 counsellor available, publications.

NSPCC (24 hours)
0800 800-500

Parentline Plus
0808 800-2222
text phone 0800 783-6783

Victim Support National Association
020 7735-9166

Websites

www.antibullying.net
Anti-Bullying Campaign
www.bullying.co.uk

Scottish Schools Ethos Network
www.ethosnet.co.uk
email ssen@education.ed.ac.uk
Faculty of Education, University of Edinburgh, Holyrood Rd, Edinburgh
EH8 8AQ

European anti-bullying project
www.gold.ac.uk/tmr/

Read more about peer support on www.guardian.unlimited.co.uk/education 28.11.00 'Lean on me' Jerome Monahan

http:pages.hotbot.com/family/famab
Families against bullying is a voluntary non profit making organisation based in England 'providing free and confidential advice and support to victims of school bullying and their families'.

Peer Support Forum
www.mentalhealth.org.uk/peer/forum.htm

www.nobully.org.nz for a New Zealand perspective

www.peacebuildersoz.com is a long term community based violence reduction/crime prevention programme. Now being tested in a Scottish primary school.

www.peersupport.co.uk
The three groups below have joined forces on this website:

CHIPS, **Childline in partnership with schools**
Mental Health Foundation
Peer support networker

Pupiline.net set up by 16 year old Oli Watts, this impressive site hosts a lively and supportive debate on bullying in which visitors share their experiences.
www.pupiline.net

Samaritans www.samaritans.org have a free teaching pack designed to help secondary schools tackle subjects such as stress, anxiety and isolation. It can be downloaded from their website.

Other resources

"On the right track"

A video and workbook resource, from 'Peacemakers with Attitude'.

Highlights the issue of bullying from different perspectives i.e. the person being bullied, the bully and the bystander.

Supported by Connections – Family Service Unit's national anti-bullying campaign. PWA West Leeds Family Service Unit,

3, Chiswick St,
Leeds LS6 7QE
Tel: 0113 275 7600
Fax: 0113 2789990
E mail: wlfsu@aol.com

Publications and Videos
Countering Bullying Unit
University of Wales Institute
Cyncoed Rd,
Cardiff, CF23 6XD
Email: mjthomas@uwic.ac.uk

Further Reading and Information

Besag, V. **'Coping with Life'** series, CD ROM **'Coping with Bullying'**
Rotary UK "Coping with Bullying" CD ROM part of the "Coping with Life" series. Free to schools, write to :

Coping With Life , PO Box 40 Ashington
NE63 8YR

Email colin@sawyer.demon,co,uk
www.sawyer.demon.co.uk

Buchanan, A. & Hudson, B. (2000) **Promoting Children's Emotional Well-being** Oxford: Oxford University Press

Clare, A. (2000) **On Men: Masculinity in Crisis** London: Chatto & Windus

Family Service Units
207 Old Marylebone Rd
London NW1 5QP Tel 0207 402 5175
Fax 0207 724 1829
Connections anti-bullying programme involving peer support and ethos change. Video, Resource book, support for schools. The **Connections Project** at Family Service Units (a national charity working at a local level with families experiencing difficulty) has been working with schools and community groups to develop non-punitive and inclusive strategies for beginning the process of preventing bullying and related behaviours.
For information on workshops please contact Dave Brown:
Family Service Units
207 Old Marylebone Rd.
London
NW1 5QP
Tel/Fax 0208 527 2847
E Mail: shad@hats3.freeserve.co.uk

Hartley-Brewer, E. (2000) **Self Esteem for Girls, 100 Tips** London: Vermilion

Hartley-Brewer, E. (2000) **Self Esteem for Boys, 100 Tips** London: Vermilion

Olweus, D. (1993) **Bullying at School: What we know and what we can do.** Oxford: Blackwell Publishers.
108 Cowley Rd Oxford Ox 1JF UK.

Olweus' core programme against bullying and anti-social behaviour: A teacher handbook. Research Centre for Health Promotion (Hemil Centre) Bergen, Norway

Olweus, D.& Limber, S. (1999) Blueprints for violence prevention: **Bullying Prevention** Programme Institute of Behavioural Science, University of Colorado Boulder USA
www.colorado.edu/cspv/blueprints

Olweus, D. (1978) **Aggression in Schools: Bullies and whipping boys.**
Washington DC: Hemisphere (Wiley)

Rigby, K. (1996) **Bullying in Australian Schools – And what to do about it.** Melbourne: ACER

Sullivan, K. (2000) **The Anti-Bullying Handbook** Oxford: Oxford University Press.

The Convention on The Rights of The Child Article 19

Wilson, P. (1996) **Mental Health in Your School** London: Jessica Kingsely.

WHAT WORKS?

Here is what Young Voice learned from practitioners and researchers, teachers and young people in the course of this study.

Within school

Shift from an 'anti-bullying' approach to a 'prevention of bullying' stance.

This has to be 'global' in reach and solution focused.

Beware of punitive patterns reinforcing the bully's emotional blueprint.

Revenge under the guise of Justice can worsen the situation

Challenge the whole school ethos.

Enlist support from the whole community

Bring in all other agencies where possible.

Tackle habitual responses – it doesn't have to be this way

Give kids and adults a reason to say Stop! There are choices to be made.

Bullying should bring no rewards to the bully, such as status, reputation and power. Girls like the reward of exclusivity – a small 'in' group. Boys like power.

Encourage young people to develop self-awareness and empathy through peer support.

Work to build confidence and resilience in all pupils.

Encourage initiative in all pupils.

Develop ethics of care and respect.

Improvements to classroom management have been shown to reduce bullying and raise standards. This can be more sustainable than blitz campaigns against bullying.

Stop pupils bullying teachers and teachers bullying pupils.

Create conditions of democratic participation, by encouraging pupils to think about their predicament. What do they want to happen?

Ensure privacy and dignity, enhancing children's sense of self-agency as opposed to victim-hood and 'effacing' treatment.

Working to enhance bullies' self-confidence without using sanctions, has not been found helpful. Sanctions however, should be non violent.

Some programmes of peer support enlist bullies positively, provided they are prevented from abusing that power.

The wider community

A violent society gives a message that the school policy has to fight against. To counter this, try to involve parents, other local schools, estates and local bus services.

Install an anonymous system of monitoring the 'temperature' within the school and its surroundings.

Bullying has long-term anti-social effects within the community, tie all efforts to the wider picture and enlist the help of police, criminal justice system, health visitors, school nurses and mental health professionals.

Big differences in exclusion rates have been found which are not attributable to catchment areas. Bullying is one indicator of behavioural problems in school. Although temperament and experience are factors, the 15000 hours a child spends in school is a key influence.

Durham County Council is leading the way with a county wide anti-bullying scheme involving all council staff. It offers training to schools.

Such a scheme can involve leisure centres, libraries, park staff and transport workers.

Provide information on helplines and supportive websites such as www.pupiline.net so that an individual can seek support privately.

Involving parents

If parents don't come to Parents' Evenings on Bullying, change the title of the meeting to 'The Rights of Your Child', for a full house.

Tell parents – no child should have this happen, no parent should be afraid of this happening to their child.

Enlist parents' support and agreement with the policy when their child starts at the school via the home/school contract.

Remind and refresh – update parents higher up in school

The largest number of parents' calls on school matters to Parentline, the helpline for parents, concern bullying.

Parentline reports that 71 of the 161 children who were being bullied were receiving some kind of therapeuetic help; half found this helpful, but the rest stopped after one or two sessions – this could be a reaction to what appears to be a long wait for help- from three months to a year.

Parents also rang Parentline for help to manage their child's bullying behaviour, saying that the school was not helping them.

Children who bully were also cause for concern for other reasons including stealing, drug and alcohol abuse, underage sex, and smoking. Strong links were recognised to changes in the child's external world – being bullied at a previous school, moving house, changing school, introduction of new partner, death of a close family member.

The view children have of adults' intervention:

Sometimes adults getting involved are seen as intimidating, intrusive, patronising or judgemental. There can be repercussions that adults are not aware of.

General principles may not be sensitive enough to provide for individual children whose needs and background vary.

Inform and empower as a matter of course. Adults tend to do so only at points of crisis. Failure to do so keeps some young people vulnerable.

Respect our civic liberties.

Make sure that an anti-bullying policy is implemented and not only in a glossy brochure or locked in a filing cabinet and used for open evenings.

Pupils want mutual recognition and respect from adults in power

Adults should help victims increase their competence and resilience. They need help to participate more.

Adults should take the time to listen.

If the programme in place is strong on care and welfare, it may nevertheless lack democratic participation if it means that adults are still deciding what's best, without young people as partners.

Some parents actively advocate violent responses.

Involve children in a 'swap places for a day' exercise, where head teacher takes the place of the child in class and the child (selected after a nomination process) takes a team of deputy and dining room manager to the task of managing the school. This idea, tried in a London primary, allows children to prepare a blueprint on 'What I would change about the school' it provokes debate and reveals to the school how children view things. Children come to think about what education should deliver, what the responsibilities are.

Acknowledgements: various items adapted from the work of:

David Brown, FSU Connections programme, Professor Dan Olweus, Dr Erling Rowland, Childline, Prof Helen Cowie, Primrose Hill primary school, Durham County Council anti bullying peer support programme. With acknowledgements to ACPP conference, Bullying In Schools. And the many peer supporters, bullies and victims who shared advice.

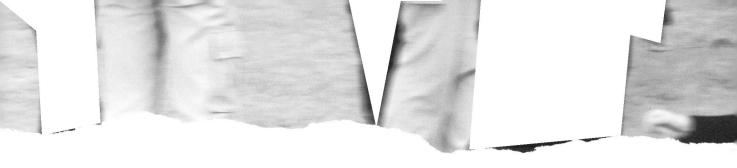

WHAT NEXT?

Bullying is a vital social indicator of the health of a community, as these testimonies from teenagers show. Now Young Voice asks - what next? If bullying is to be reduced - along with its effect on depression, juvenile offending, blighting children's futures and relations between diverse communities – a fully rounded response is required.

Young people have told us that around half of their schools still don't have an anti-bullying policy. Of those who do, only around a half are said to be effective. One in ten pupils experience severe bullying including physical violence.

Schools should be encouraged to embrace the information available to them from the DfEE and beyond. Research shows how improving the school ethos and group dynamics within the classroom and the school campus, can raise standards in many ways across the school. There are excellent programmes available from the voluntary sector and within the educational establishment that can be called upon. Training and resources are available. A multi agency approach should involve local transport companies, police and representatives from other schools, estates and youthworkers.

Sustainability is key as bullying rates appear to drift upwards once more some time after successful implementation. Involving the pupils democratically is essential.

But schools cannot do it alone. They operate within a community. Parents' co-operation must be obtained when a child begins at a school. They must sign up to the values of the policy and agree to support it. They must understand what the school community will not tolerate.

Work with parents on developing positive parenting and reducing violence towards children is seen as an integral part of the action required - too many young people shockingly report being hit, beaten or experiencing violence from an adult.

Young people's mental and emotional health should be a priority within the curriculum and in improved professional services. The levels of depression and suicidal thoughts are worrying.

Teaching conflict resolution, anger management and respect for others can only take place in a context in which children are not bullied by adults but play a full part with adults in negotiating anti-bullying strategies and developing peer support.

Most of all, this project shows how important it is to consult children in the development and monitoring of any anti bullying policy and to do this regularly and with each new intake.

Adrienne Katz
Young Voice January 2001

Notes